# THE BIG CLIMB

How the world's toughest road race created a nation of cycling superstars

Stephen Norman

The author is grateful to the Biblioteca Pública Piloto, of Medellín, Colombia for their permission to publish the many photographs of Horacio Gil Ochoa to be found in this work.

This first edition is published in 2019 by
Smiths Hall Publishing
Smiths Hall
West Farleigh,
Maidstone,
ME15 0PE,
United Kingdom

ISBN-13: 978-1-9162489-0-8

Author: Stephen Norman
Production & video: Pamela Gowland
Graphic design: Lalo Quintana, Barcelona
Printed and bound by: www.cegeglobal.com

The mountains of Colombia
have bred generations
of cycling champions.
This book, packed with
180 photographs, maps,
diagrams and links to
historical movie clips,
explains how the
Vuelta a Colombia
gripped the imagination
of a nation and created
– and continues to foster –
some of the finest cyclists
the world has ever seen.

Author: Stephen Norman
Production & video: Pamela Gowland
Graphic design: Lalo Quintana

Horacio Gil Ochoa (1930 – 2018) *Biblioteca Publica Piloto, Medellin*

Front cover photo by Horacio Gil Ochoa, from the 1963 Vuelta a Colombia.

On the back of the print, Ochoa wrote: *"This ford between Supia and La Pintada was a great place for photos. Few riders could cross without getting off. But on this day, one of them was Cochise, and he looked triumphant."*

And indeed Martín Emilio Rodríguez, ('Cochise') - seen in the foreground - led the race from this stage onwards to final victory in Bogota, 8 days later.

Father and son.
*Photo Esteban Chaves*

# FOREWORD BY ESTEBAN CHAVES

Esteban Chaves is a professional Colombian cyclist. His many victories include the Tour de l'Avenir (2011), 2nd place in the Giro d'Italia (2016) and 3rd in the Vuelta a España (2016). He currently rides for the Australian team, Mitchelton-Scott.

*As long as I can remember, cycling was always part of my life. Since I was a kid, my dad made me fall completely in love with the bike and made me dream of becoming a professional cyclist one day.*

*Unlike most Colombian professional cyclists, I was born - on January 17th, 1990 - and raised in the capital city of Bogotá, among 7 million other inhabitants. At home, I grew up hearing the fantastic and heroic stories of Alfonso Flórez and Martín Ramírez, conquering Tour de l'Avenir, and I watched images and vintage videos of Lucho Herrera and Fabio Parra taking our country to the top, to the podium of the Tour de France and Vuelta a España. These golden years of Colombian cycling made my dad a crazy fan of this sport and this passion became a key part of my family life.*

*I remember my childhood full of bikes, wheels, helmets, cycling gear, with races always on TV, and cycling magazines pasted on the walls. I will never forget the incredible moments I watched on TV: Santiago Botero becoming World Champion, Víctor Hugo Peña wearing the yellow jersey for the first time in Colombian history, Iván Parra winning those mythic stages in the Italian Dolomites while riding for Colombia-Selle Italia, and Luis Felipe Laverde, climbing and winning at the Giro d'Italia.*

*When I was 13 years old, I started to ride and these great deeds convinced me that my dreams of becoming a pro cyclist, of riding in the Grand Tours and winning the Tour de France, were possible. They inspired me to work harder every day and overcome difficult times. They were part of my process and they are part of who I am today.*

*Now, at 29 years of age, I can say that most of my dreams have come true, I am actually living one of my biggest dreams, which was to ride for one of the best cycling teams in the world and I am on my way to achieve many more. Although it is a hard sport, cycling changed not only my life but that of my family and people close to me. It gave us unforgettable moments, taught us important lessons and instilled in us life values. Values such as tenacity, optimism and perseverance that reflect Colombian culture.*

The FUN Foundation

*Colombia is a country full of sporting talent and warrior souls. There are plenty of children that have the same dreams as I had when I was 13 years old.*

*For this reason, we created FUN Esteban Chaves, a nonprofit organization that aims to inspire talented youngsters to pursue and achieve their dreams. My father is the general director, and he continues to spread love and passion for this sport as he did with me and my brother, years ago.*

*Colombian cycling, and especially its success on the professional level is still a mystery to the world but for me, is a matter of family, dreams and legacy. But to understand this mystery, we should start with its history and origins. This book with its wonderful illustrations takes us back in time and explains how it all began. If you love cycling as much as I do, you will enjoy every page.*

Esteban Chaves

You can learn more about Esteban, his ambitions and his family in this video.

# WHY
# THE BIG CLIMB?

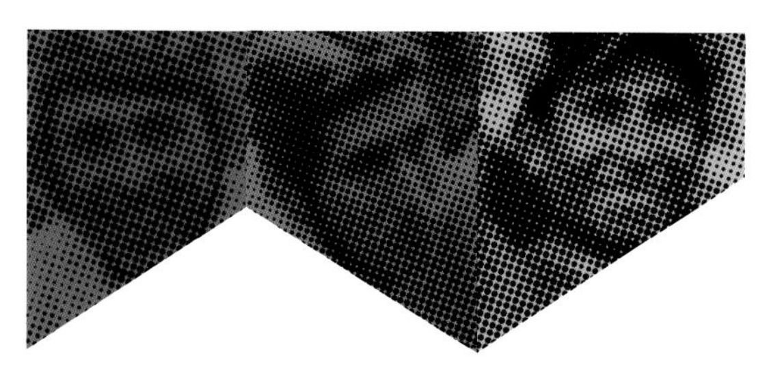

A year ago, I was researching for a book, a novel, to be set over the course of a Grand Tour cycle race. I spent hours watching the big races on TV (it's all work, you know). I was struck by the success of Colombian riders. Gaviria, Urán, Pantano, Henao, Chaves, Bernal, Anacona, and of course the great Nairo Quintana. All winning races.

It set me thinking. What was their secret? Why not México or Perú or Argentina or the USA? What the heck was going on back there *in Colombia*?

**Was I imagining it? Look at this chart!**

These Colombians are out-performing the rest of Latin America *combined.*
Here's another statistic: in the decade since 2010, young Colombians have won the Tour de l'Avenir (the prestigious European race for under-23s) *four times*: Nairo Quintana in 2010, Esteban Chaves in 2011, Miguel Ángel López in 2014 and finally Egan Bernal in 2017.

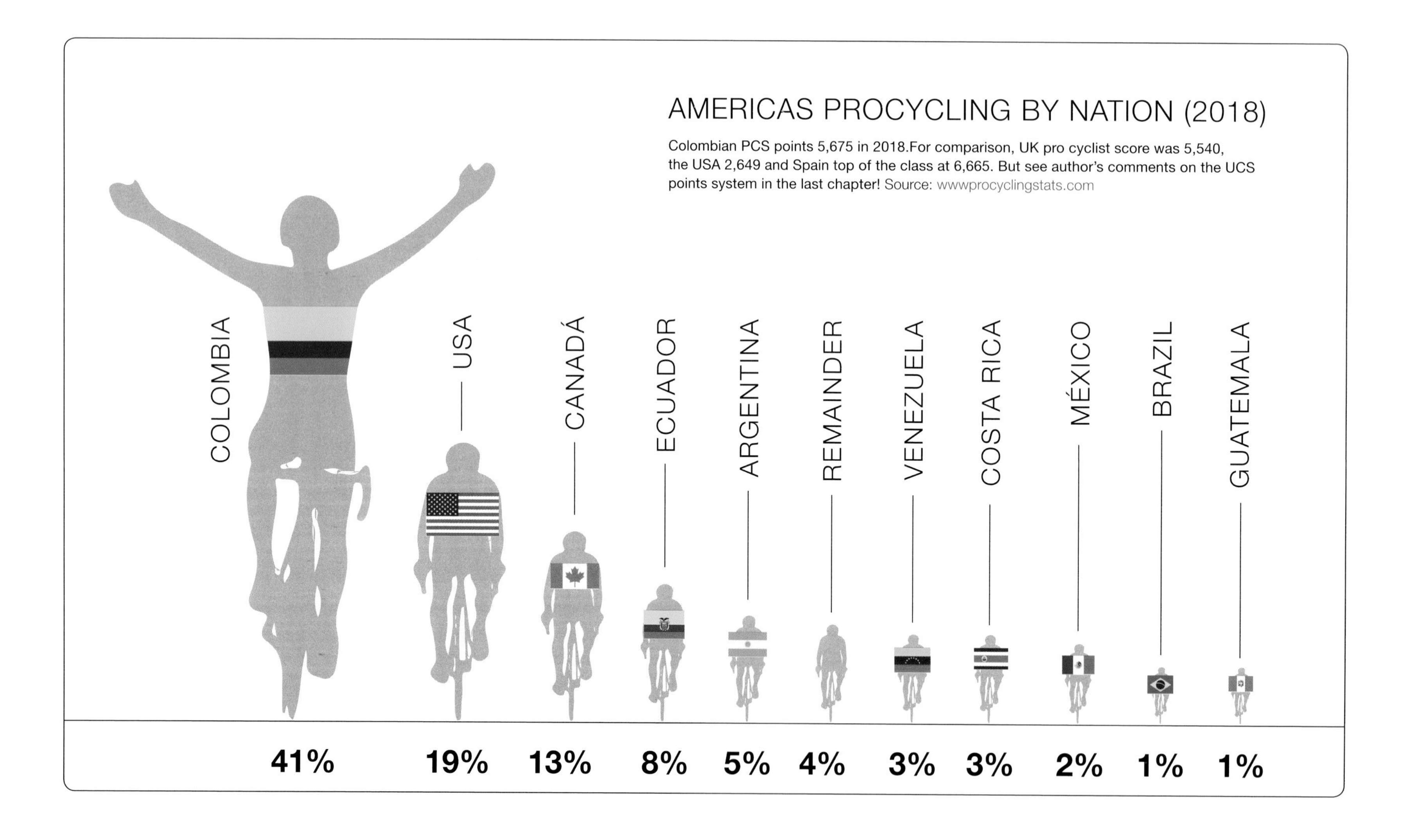

Against the best in the world, for the Tour de l'Avenir is truly "the race of the future". Those same four Colombians have between them won all three Grand Tours, and stood on the podium of those Grand Tours *11 times*.

I started looking for answers. It was frustrating. There is not a lot on Colombian cycling, and especially not in English. As a result, the European cycling fraternity, that army of enthusiasts who pedal all over Europe and wear badges showing how many times they climbed Mont Ventoux in a day, know nothing about Colombian road racing, and its origins.

I offer this book as a humble antidote to the mystery! It tells the story of Colombia's love affair with bike racing through words, pictures and the occasional map or graph. It is a history with a lot of facts and little anecdotes. It is not a tome, it is not a 'coffee table' book, it's a 'bedside table' book, meant to lie around and entertain[1].

You might say "it's the mountains!" But you know, those countries all share the Andes – or the Rockies.

Of course the mountains have a role, but that's not enough. To understand the phenomenon that is Colombian cycling, we need to go back in time, to 1951, when a race called the "Vuelta a Colombia" ("Tour of Colombia") was born.

1. If you crave more detail, more political context, more oomph, after perusing these pages, then buy, borrow or steal Kings of the Mountains by Matt Rendell. This fascinating book covers the history of Colombian cycling, and explains how it has influenced the social and political history of the nation.

"The roads were just tracks in those days." *BPP, Medellin*

In that year, 35 intrepid souls gathered on their bikes outside the offices of El Tiempo in Bogota. What they were going to attempt was crazy, I mean really crazy. They were going to cycle from Bogota across the country, up and down climbs higher and longer than anything you will find in the Alps or the Pyrenees.

And the roads! They were just tracks in those days, with huge ruts made by the trucks. When it rained, they turned to mud. When it was dry, they turned to dust.

*"Roads? What roads?"*
Early footage of the dreadful state of the roads, amusingly narrated by the doyen of Colombian sports commentators, Carlos Arturo Rueda.

The bikes of these 35 intrepid souls were not like today's bikes. They were mostly home-grown and made of steel. Every so often, the front forks or the headset would snap, which isn't fun at 90 kilometres an hour downhill. The tyres weren't up to much either.

It wasn't unusual for a rider to have half a dozen punctures in one day.

These crazies were going to risk their lives for 10 days over 1,157 kilometres of bad road. Everyone in Colombia was going to know about it, because the press was right behind the venture. *El Tiempo* (think *"The Times"*) was sponsoring it and a small army of radio commentators was going to broadcast it. And they succeeded! In the early years of the Vuelta a Colombia, 150,000 people would welcome their heroes home to Bogota. Country folks would walk miles, just to cheer those crazies going by.

The Vuelta a Colombia captured the imagination of the nation. Not just as spectators. Every farm boy in the mountains, every bicycle messenger on the steep streets of Medellín or Bogotá could dream of winning the Vuelta, and every year, one of them did. And still does. I believe it was that race, that accident of history, that led the Colombian people to their love affair with cycling. And the mountains, of course. And the politics.

# THE MOUNTAINS

One needs two maps and a short geography lesson to follow the history of Colombian cycling, with all its sweat, pain and bitter rivalry. On the right is the first of them: the physical geography.

Look at those mountains! The Andes form a mighty wall up the west coast of South America, from Chile through Bolivia, Perú and Ecuador. But where they cross the border into the south of Colombia, they split into three ranges or cordilleras, like the three middle fingers of a hand.

The Oriental (eastern) and Central cordilleras are the highest and broadest, and in between them flows the Magdalena River, which runs northwards into the Caribbean Sea. The capital city of Bogota sits on a plateau on the edge of the eastern cordillera. The Occidental (western) cordillera is thinner, and clings tight alongside the Central. The cities of Cali and Medellin nestle in-between the Central and Occidental cordilleras (see map).

The mountains of the Occidental cordillera go up to 4,000 metres (12,400 feet), which is a decent height. But there are mountains in the Central and Eastern cordilleras over 5,000 metres (15,500 feet) and the peaks are permanently snow covered. There are many passes and roads over 3,000 metres, including some famous ones that generations of Colombian cyclists have fought over.

The valleys between the cordilleras are as low as the mountains are high. The city of Honda, for example, on the broad Magdalena River, appears often in the history of the Vuelta. It is 850 kilometres upriver from the sea but just 229 metres above sea level. **IT IS HOT.**

A large percentage of the country lives on the high plateaus, especially that around Bogota. Even the second city, Medellin, is at an altitude of 1,495 metres and the mountains rise to 3,000 metres on all sides.

Unlike the Alps, where the upland pastures are snow covered during the winter, inhabited only by farmers and winter sports fans, the uplands of Colombia are more temperate. The snow level is consistently at 5,000 metres or 16,500 feet, whereas the snow level of the Alps in summer is c. 3,000 metres. This mountainous geography, and especially its high uplands, form a natural breeding ground for our cyclists.

Young Colombians not only learn to climb big hills, but they live at high altitudes and develop exceptional lung and oxygen carrying capacity.

The Colombian cycling legend Nairo Quintana (or just 'Nairo' to any Colombian) was born and raised in a farmhouse in Boyaca, at 3,200 metres (10,560 feet). He used to cycle 16 kilometres (10 miles) down to school, and 16 kilometres back up. The climb home was 725 metres (2,400 feet). Good training!

The mountains define the physical geography. One also needs the political geography to follow the story.

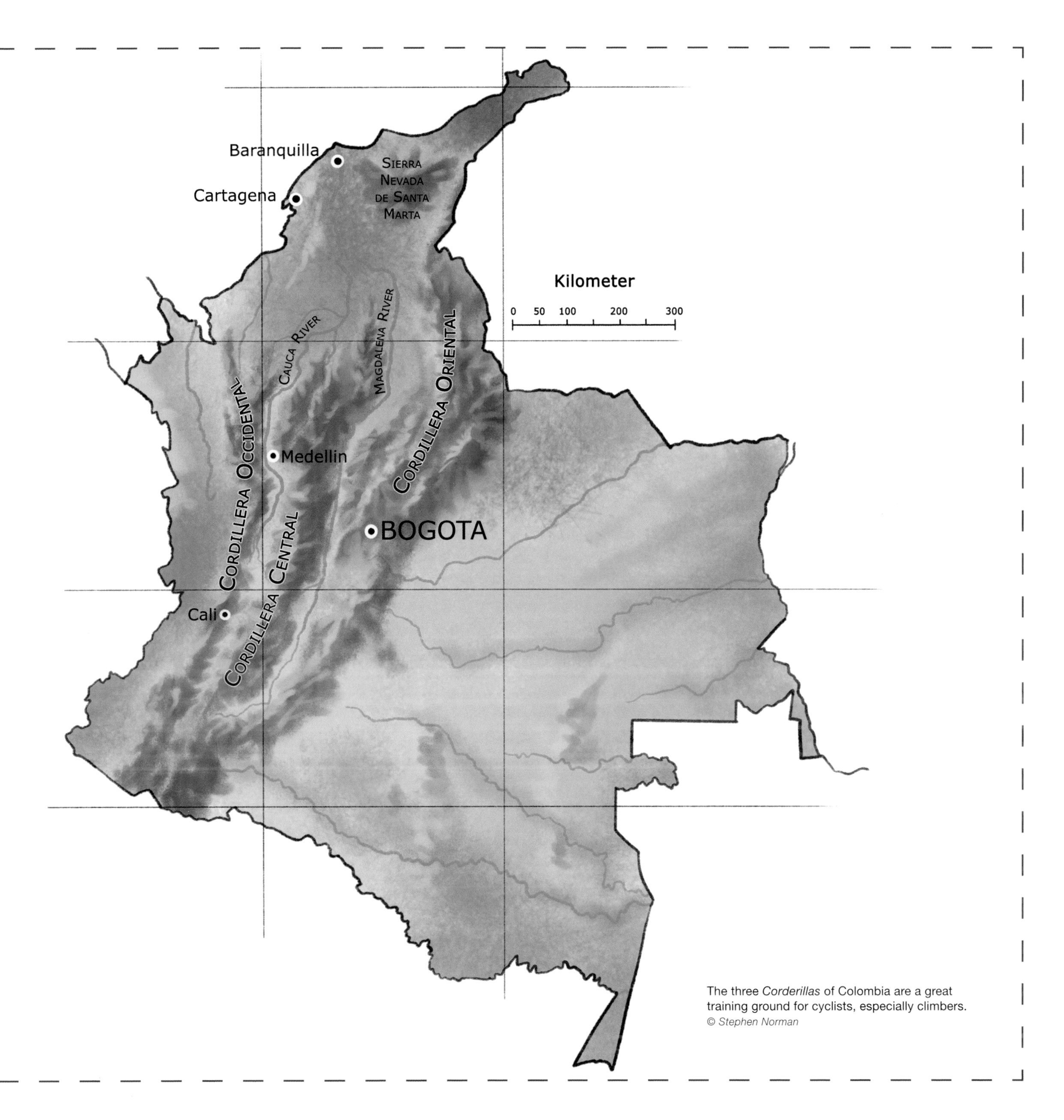


The three *Corderillas* of Colombia are a great training ground for cyclists, especially climbers.
*© Stephen Norman*

# THE POLITICS

| DEPARTMENT | GC WINS |
|---|---|
| Boyacá | 26 |
| Antioquia | 16 |
| Cundinamarca | 8 |
| Santander | 6 |
| Caldas | 3 |
| Tolima | 1 |
| Bogotá | 1 |

Colombia is made up of departments, which are like states or counties. There are 32 of them and a federal capital (Bogotá). Each department has a capital, an assembly and its own provincial governor.

History and geography combine to give each department a distinctive cultural identity. Each of them has its own typical costumes, cuisine, flag and in many cases a distinctive accent.

In the early days of the Vuelta, there was fierce rivalry between departments, and especially between Antioquia and its three rivals on the Oriental corderilla: Boyacá, Santander and Cundinamarca. Apart from the 7 foreign wins, these 4 departments have won 56 of the 61 victories in the General Classification. On the map, you can see that these departments spread over the high uplands of the Central and Oriental corderillas.

But come and see for yourself! Colombia is a beautiful, welcoming country, especially to cyclists. You may have been up the Alpe d'Huez or Mt. Ventoux but so have all your friends! When you have been over the Alto de Letras or the Alto de Minas, you will have – and you will deserve – some special bragging rights.

P.S. Most people have heard of Pablo Escobar. But did you know that his older brother Roberto was an elite cyclist? This is not a book about politics, but to understand what happened to Colombian cycling in the 1980s and 1990s, it's necessary to talk about the drugs, the money and the politics. Which we do, in the later sections of this book.

Four mountainous departments of Colombia dominate the cycling scene. © *Stephen Norman*

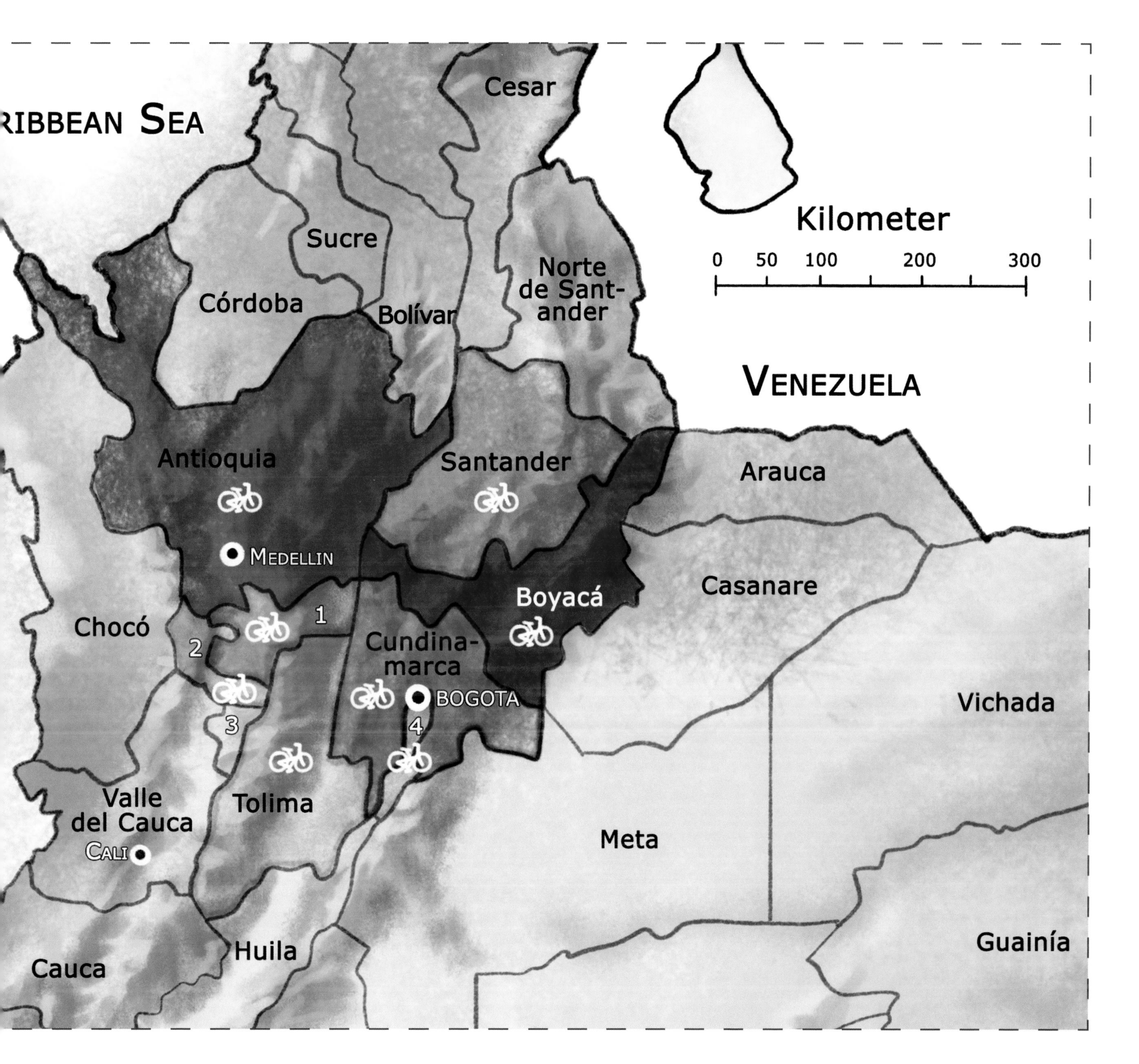

RIBBEAN SEA
Cesar
Kilometer
0
50
100
200
300
Sucre
Norte de Sant-ander
Córdoba
Bolívar
VENEZUELA
Antioquia
Santander
Arauca
MEDELLIN
Casanare
Boyacá
1
Chocó
2
Cundina-marca
BOGOTA
Vichada
3
4
Valle del Cauca
Tolima
Meta
CALI
Huila
Guainía
Cauca

# VISITING COLOMBIA

Colombia welcomes all visitors, and especially those on two wheels. The roads are good and the mountain biking awesome, but you need advice about how to avoid the trucks. Here are some enthusiasts who can help.

IN COLOMBIA:

**ABC Bike Tour Colombia**
Single and multiday bike and adventure tours around and in the coffee farms and hills of Quindio

+57 310 506 1613
bookings@biketourcolombia.com

**Casa du Velo Cycling Hotel**
Lots of multiday tours around the coffee growing region of Quindio based from their Cycling Hotel

+57 300 462 44 00
book@casaduvelo.com

**Cyclota.com**
Multiday road tours including some of the great climbs, Bogota, Medellin, coffee country

+57 316 8334072
info@cyclota.com

**Colombian Bike Junkies**
On and off road biking, rafting and hiking in several cities:

San Gil +57 316 327 6101
info@colombianbikejunkies.com
Bogota +57 301 473 2853
bogota@colombianbikejunkies.com
Medellin +57 318 808 6769
medellin@colombianbikejunkies.com

**Colombia Cycling**
Wide ranging multiday bike tours in Antioquia, Medellin and up the Alto de Letras

+57 314 7176809
info@colombiacycling.com

## OVERSEAS OPERATORS

**Pure (Colombia)**
Tailor-made cycling programs around Colombia (road and mountain bike).

+57 316 407 2732
info@pure-colombia.com

**Gregario**
Medellin based outfit which organises road bike tours: short climbs around Medellin and multiday tours all over Colombia including Antioquia, Boyacá and the Alto de Letras.
info@gregario.co

**2000m Descent**
Exhilarating mountain biking tours around Medellin including the eponymous 2000 metres descent!

+57 313 603 9168
reservations@2000mdescent.com

**Beyond Andes Cycling and Trail Running Tours** (NZ)
Organises 19,10, 8 and 5 day tours. The 19 and 10 days tours include 2 days following the Tour Colombia! Also other Andean multiday/MTB tours eg to Perú, Bolivia.
anthony@beyondandes.com

**Saddle Skedaddle Ltd** (UK)
UK based but experienced organiser of multiday road tours around Colombia.

+44 191 265 1110
info@skedaddle.com

**Redspokes Adventure Tours** (UK),
UK based but offering adventure cycling for groups of 6 – 16 around Colombia taking in big climbs.

+44 20 7502 7252
office@redspokes.co.uk

Note: most of these operators have websites as indicated by their email addresses.

# Acknowledgements

Most of the field research for this book was done during a visit to Colombia during the 2018 Vuelta a Colombia, arranged by one of us (Pamela Gowland). During that time many busy people made time to talk to us about their life and history, starting with Pamela's friend Mario Sabato, who gave generously of his time and made many introductions. Through Mario, we met Martín Emilio "Cochise" Rodríguez, Jesus "Chucho" Piedrahita, Rafael Antonio Niño, Victor Hugo Peña, Dr Camilo Ernesto Pardo Poveda, Fabio Parra, Hernando Gaviria, Jairo "Maravilloso" Garzon, Jorge Ovidio Gonzalez and Professor Restrepo.

On our subsequent visit in 2019, the archivists of Colombia were kind to us: Danilo Pizarro (El Tiempo), Jaime Jaramillo, German Espinal and Monica Maria Arango Zapata (El Colombiano) and Jackeline Garcia Chaverra (Biblioteca Publica Piloto) all opened their vaults and allowed us to reproduce the illustrations and articles you see in these pages. Thank you.

Also our thanks to Hector Urrego Caballero, that legend of Colombian reportage, to his children and to his brother Alberto, for their help with numerous introductions, and in sourcing some of the images which appear in this book. Hector, we apologise for the interviews in terrible Spanish which we gave on RCN!

Jorge Ovidio Gonzalez, President of the Colombian Cycling Federation, was gracious in welcoming us and answering our questions, and Eder Garces Herrera, also of the Federation, helped set up the trip and the interviews.

For their insights into the recent history of Colombian cycling, we are indebted to Professor Gustavo Duncan and Ignacio Velez. Thanks also to Ernesto Lucena Barrero,the Director of Coldeportes for sharing his thoughts on the future.

Sadly, we were too late to meet Horacio Gil Ochoa, whose photography illuminates every chapter of this book. Ochoa was prolific but most of his images appeared – and then disappeared – in newsprint. The Biblioteca Pública Piloto of Medellín published his visual autobiography, *"Mi Bicicleta, Mi Camara y Yo"*. But today you cannot acquire it, neither for love nor money, but only through the generosity of Jesús Chucho Piedrahita who brought it to dinner and let us borrow it. Again with his help, we were warmly welcomed by Ochoa's son Juan and family and spent a happy day going through their family collection. Many of the forgotten prints we saw that day are reproduced here.

Thank you to Klaus Bellon for his permission to reproduce extracts from his excellent blog Alps & Andes (www.alpsandes.com) and for his help with the inside story of Colombian cycling since 2005.

Colombian cyclists are fortunate to have Alps & Andes, and also lucky to have http://altimetriascolombia.blogspot.com, the most fabulous collection of Colombian climbs, comment and cycling rants. Thank you, Gustavo Duncan and Asier Bilbao, for allowing us to reproduce some of your altimetrías and some comments on the great climbs. We enjoyed your description of the Alto de Minas from La Pintada: *"42 kilometres of complete torture."* Gustavo and Asier have recently distilled their wisdom into a book, *"Altimetrías de Colombia: los puertos donde se han forjado los escarabajos."*
Thanks also to Tomás Castrillón and Sander Bennink of Cyclota.com and Tomas and Marcela of Colombia Cycling.com for allowing us to reproduce the stylish photographs taken during their organised cycling tours of Colombia.

The roadmaps of the Vuelta were created by Yoko Matsuoka of Nasu-shiobara, Japan and the topographical images by James Middleton of Turning Turnip, UK.

QR codes are scattered through this book.
Use a QR reader app to show you old film from the archives of Señal Memoria, a Colombian institution with a treasure trove of historic films and images. But this one above is a modern introduction to this book from that giant of Colombian cycling, Martin Emilio Rodriguez, aka *Cochise.*

We are very grateful to Santiago Rocha Uribe of Señal Memoria and his Director, Jaime Humberto Silva, for their enthusiastic and patient help with tracking down old footage in their archives, and also to Valentin Bullrich Santander for his tireless dedication to the moving image.

*Stephen Norman & Pamela Gowland*

Freskola

## THE BIG CLIMB

1950 - 1960 • COLOMBIA FALLS IN LOVE

1961 - 1969 • COCHISE, COCHISE, COCHISE

1970 - 1979 • NEW KID IN TOWN

1980 - 1989 • GLORY DAYS

1990 - 1996 • ISOLATION & DECLINE

1997 - 2016 • WHOSE TURN IS IT ANYWAY?

2006 - 2019 • TOMORROW BELONGS TO ME

# Cundinamarca: home of El Zipa

Cundinamarca lies on the cordillera Oriental and surrounds the capital Bogota. Like Boyacá, it is partly Andean with rolling hills over 2,500 metres but on the western side it drops down thousands of feet to a long border along the River Magdalena.

It is a rural department with extensive agriculture, and Bogota in its centre is a ready market for its products. At the lower levels, there are coffee plantations, and higher up there are flower and orchid farms, potatoes, and lots of animals: chickens, cows and pigs.

Just to the north of Bogota lies the town of Zipaquira, famous for its salt mines and the salt cathedral, hollowed out underground, complete with chapels, altars and the stations of the Cross, all carved out of the rock.

To the east of Bogota lie lush forests and the towering waterfalls of El Chiflón and La Chorrera (the country's tallest) and the national park of Chingaza.

Chingaza is on the eastern side of the Cordillera Oriental and its lakes and rivers flow into the Orinoco Basin. The highest point in the park is 4,000 metres and the lowest is 300 metres. Chingaza is home to many animals, including spectacled bear, deer, tapirs, pumas, Andean condors, Cock-of-the-rocks birds, jaguars, turkeys, monkeys, ocelots, and toucan.

Excellent roads among rolling hills... *Photo Cyclota.com*

### *Cycling notes*

*Zipaquira is the birthplace of the founder of the Vuelta, Efraín Forero, who worked here in the soda works for most of his life. His father ran a pharmacy in the town.*

*The town of Fusagasuga, on the other side of Bogota, is the birthplace of a constellation of Colombian riders, including Lucho Herrera.*

*The Vuelta and the Clásico RCN – when they started in Bogota – left and returned to Bogota through tough climbs up from the Magdalena river. They have charming names: the Alto de Trigo, the Alto del Vino and el Alto de la Tribuna.*

The Alto de Verjon near Bogota
*Photo Cyclota.com*

# 1950-1960 COLOMBIA FALLS IN LOVE

## 1950 The Editor, the Englishman and Efraín

Amateur riders waiting at the start of a local race. It was a winning a race like this which launched el Zipa on his long career and changed the course of Colombian cycling.
*Biblioteca Publica Piloto, Medellin*

Efraín Forero:
"Why can't we have a Tour of Colombia like the Tour de France?"
*Biblioteca Publica Piloto, Medellin*

Our story begins on August 3rd, 1948. A young man from the salt mining town of Zipaquira, high up on the cordillera Oriental, shows up at the start of a local bike race. He is wearing football boots and riding a touring bike and some of the other riders make fun of him. Which makes him angry. He vows to beat them all, which he does. The prize is a wristwatch, which he will proudly display for the rest of his life.

Neither he nor his chastened tormentors yet know it, but on this day a legend was born.

The young man's name was Efraín Forero. By 1950, he had earned a place in Colombia's national cycling team. He and his teammates won a gold medal at the Pan American games in 1950.

Naturally his nickname – and most Colombian riders have nicknames – was El Zipa. *"Why,"* El Zipa asked himself, *"can Colombia not have its own Tour, like the Tour de France or the Tour (Vuelta) of Spain?"*

# The tragedy of the Nevado del Ruiz

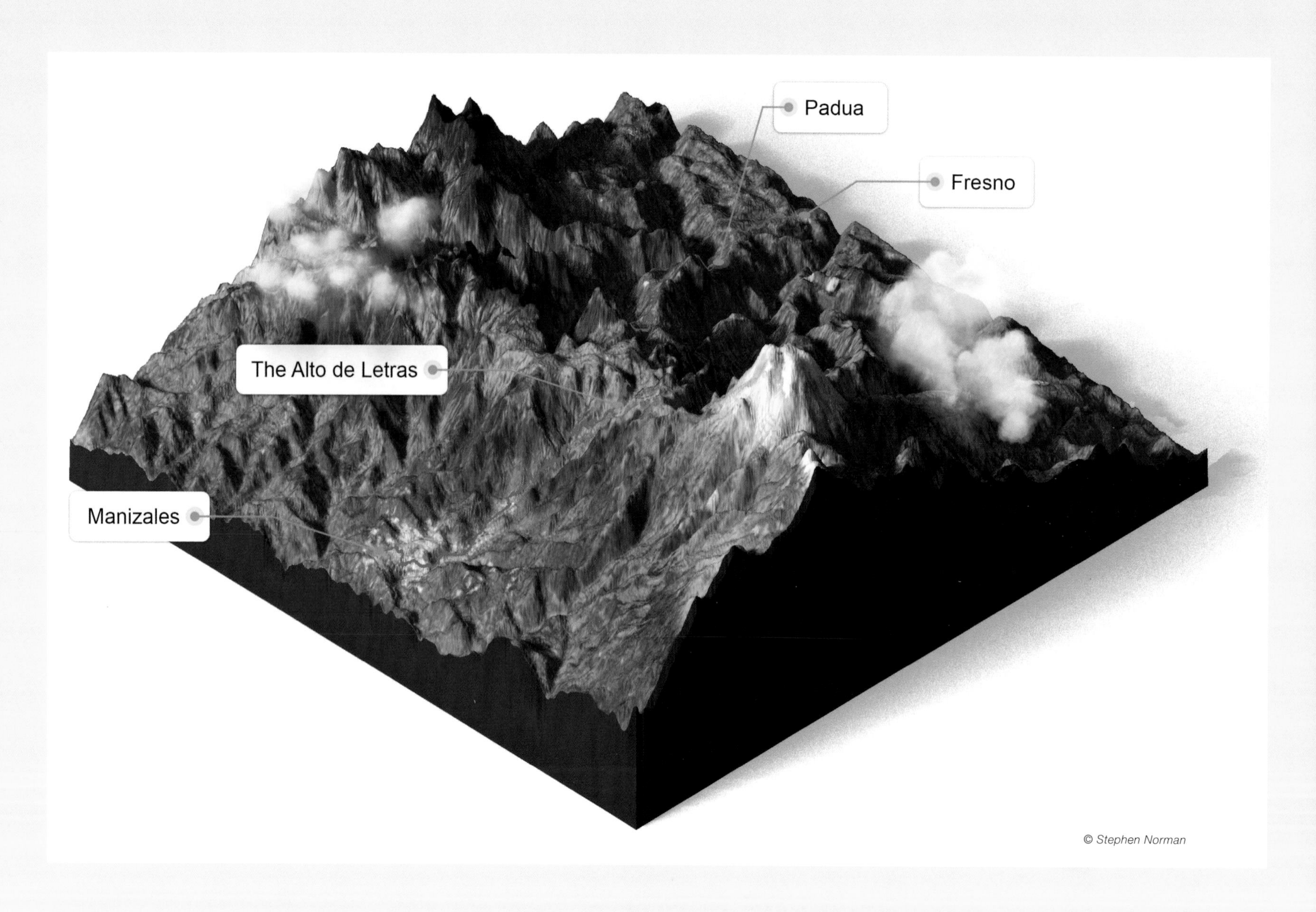


The 3,400 meters ascent of the Alto de Letras is the traditional Queen stage of the Vuelta a Colombia. The snow covered Nevado del Ruiz (17,420ft) towers above the pass.

In 1985 it erupted. Huge lahars – rivers of mud and lava – surged down the valleys to the east. 23,000 people and the town of Armero were buried under the mud.

# 1950 The Editor, the Englishman and Efraín

Forero discussed this idea with his friend Pablo Camacho Montoya, a sports journalist on El Tiempo, one of Colombia's leading newspapers. By a happy coincidence, the editor of El Tiempo was not only a keen cyclist but also President of the Colombian Cycling Association. The proposition appealed to him, and also to the secretary of the Association, an Englishman called Donald Raskin.

These three agreed to back the idea – if Forero could prove that the course was feasible. Their concerns were not academic.

Donald Raskin (left) was the secretary of the Colombian Cycling Federation. An able organiser, he would appear at the finish, waving the chequered flag and holding a stopwatch - always neatly dressed in jacket and tie. *Biblioteca Publica Piloto, Medellin*

The three Andean corderillas were daunting barriers, especially since the roads over them were unpaved and deeply rutted by rain and trucks. The low country between the mountains was tropical, hot and humid. And back then, the country was governed by a right wing dictator, Laureano Gómez, who was busy pursuing an anti-Communist purge in which many were executed without trial.

But Efraín Forero was determined. To show what could be done, he proposed to ride solo over the most difficult stage of the proposed cycle route, crossing the Central cordillera from Honda to Manizales.

Honda is a small, swelteringly hot town on the banks of the Magdalena River, at an altitude of 229 metres. The highest point on the road is the Alto de Letras, at an altitude of 3,679 metres above mean sea level. The climb therefore exceeds 3,400 metres or 11,000 feet, and is followed by a swift descent to Manizales at 2,107 metres.

Mud, rocks, rivers and steep slopes
*Casa Editorial El Tiempo S.A.*

So one fine day in October, 1950, Forero set out from Honda. Donald Raskin, the secretary of the Cycling Association, and another enthusiast, Remolacho Martinez, followed in a pickup truck. The road was so bad and so steep that the truck could not keep up. The photo below, taken during the 1952 Vuelta, helps us to imagine the scene.

Halfway up the driver wanted to give up, but Efraín Forero went on climbing, alone. Shaking with cold and covered in mud, he crossed the Alto de Letras and descended into legend. He arrived in Manizales, two hours ahead of Raskin and the truck! The astonished citizens of Manizales carried him, shoulder high, around the town.

Efraín Forero relives the deal – and the ordeal – which gave birth to the first Vuelta a Colombia.

# The Climbs of Colombia

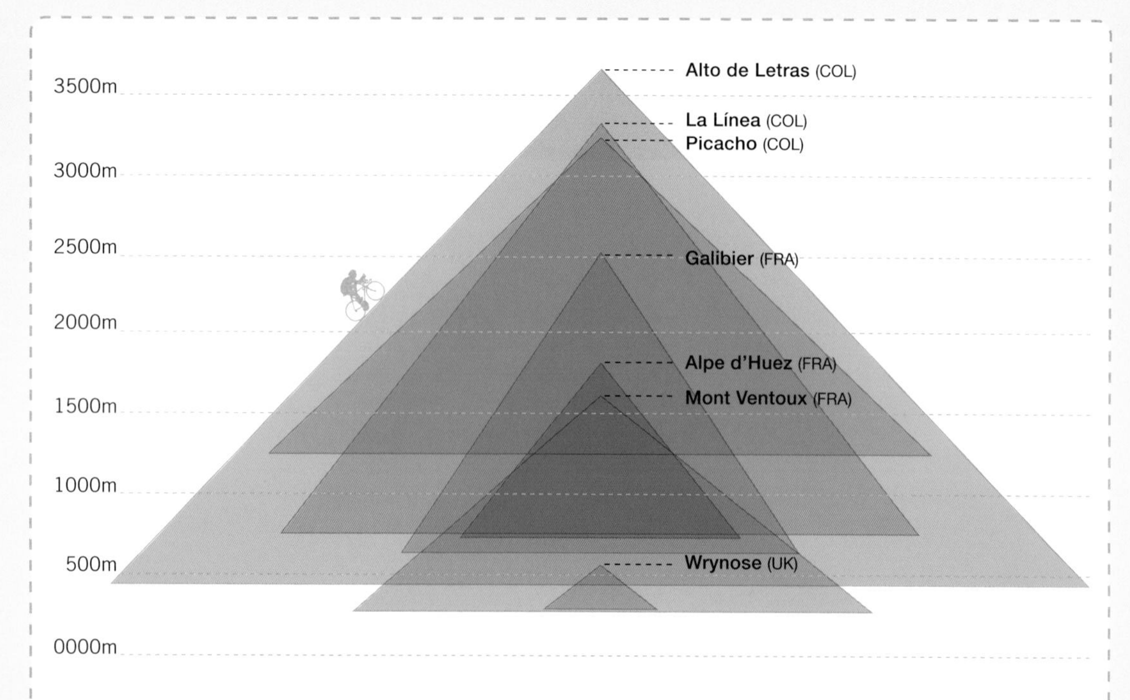


The base of each triangle marks the altitude of the start of the climb. The width of the triangle is the length. By the time you get to the top of Ventoux, you are not even halfway up Letras! PS. You might find little Wrynose in the UK Peak District amusing, but not when you get to the 33% section!

*© Stephen Norman*

Lucho Herrera, one of the greatest of Colombian cyclists, once said that Colombian riders would need a complete change of style to succeed in Europe. What did he mean? "The climbs are too short," was the laconic answer. Enigmatic, even nonsense, to the European rider. After all, it is 28 hard kilometres from Aigueblanche to the Col de Telegraphe. How can that be too short?

But Herrera was speaking the truth. Compared to the Alps or the Pyrenees, the great Colombian climbs are much longer and higher. The Alto de Letras, which for many years was the first big climb of the Vuelta, starts below 500 metres and finishes at 3,679 metres (over 12,000 feet).

On the other hand, the Colombian gradient is typically less extreme (not always!) and the ascents are less prone to sudden changes of pitch than their alpine cousins.

There are in general fewer hairpins and more long straights. In the early days of the Vuelta, these roads were unpaved roller-coasters, pitted with ruts created by logging trucks and tropical rain. Descending on the straight at 90 kilometres an hour was terrifyingly dangerous. Cornering at speed with the precipice waiting below was equally dangerous. Every year there were deaths or serious accidents.

On his famous solo ride over Letras in 1950, Efraín Forero was said to have arrived in Manizales **two and a half hours** before his support team in the pickup.
The picture below gives some clues as to how that was possible!

A FALTA DE AUTOPISTA BUENO ES EL LODO

*Pese a las noticias en contrario de la prensa oficial, las carreteras no son como se las ha querido pintar. Por el contrario, lodazales impresionantes, aunque no se ha presentado un invierno fuerte, estorban el paso de los esforzados ciclistas. Aquí vemos a la camioneta de uno de los participantes varada en una enorme charca. Con la ayuda de gran cantidad de gente se logró volverla a poner en marcha por la "autopista" que une a Riosucio con Pereira, en cuyo trayecto se captó esta gráfica. — (Foto Sady, vía Avianca).*

The headline reads "WHERE THERE IS NO ROAD, THERE IS PLENTY OF MUD." *Casa Editorial El Tiempo S.A.*

# 1951 Triumph of the indomitable Zipa

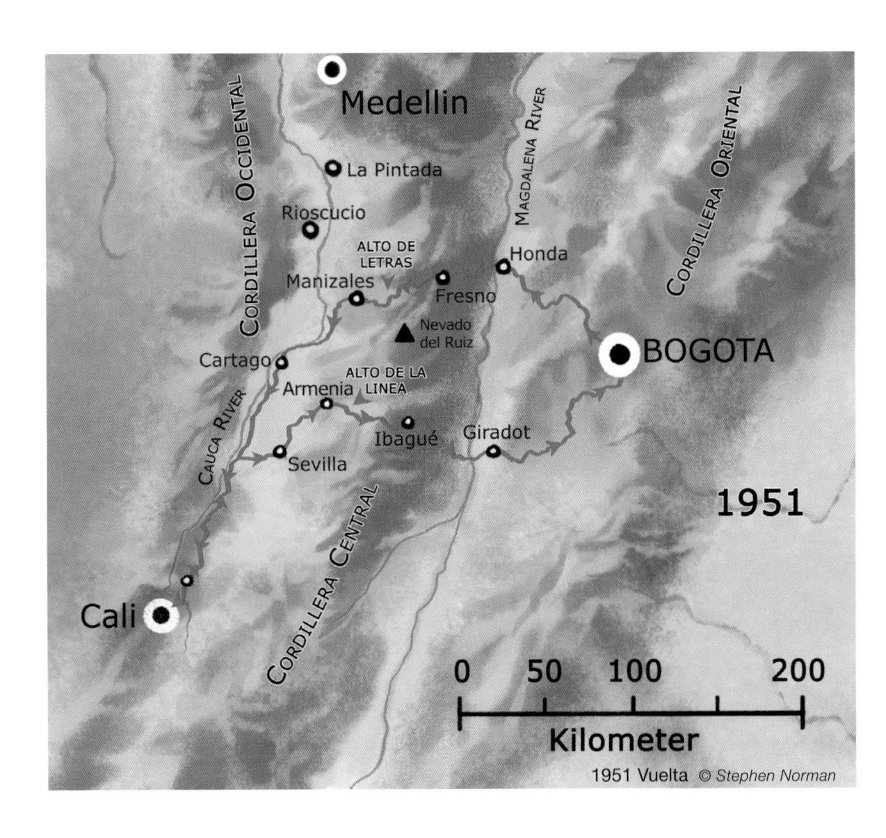

1951 Vuelta © Stephen Norman

The third stage was the ascent of Alto de Letras, the same climb that Forero had undertaken to prove the feasibility of the project. Heavy rain battered the climbers all the way to the top at 3,679 metres, and then harsh sunshine on the way down. A leading Antioquian cyclist, Nel Gil, and Efraín Forero went over the top together. Then Forero crashed and cut his knee. His mother – who was his support assistant – urged him back on his bike. He continued the descent, passing Nel Gil whose front wheel had collapsed!

The radio commentator Carlos Arturo Rueda was moved by his extraordinary resilience to christen him “indomitable”.

## The name stuck and the “Indomitable Zipa” was born.

Carlos Arturo Rueda explains how the first Vueltas were run on a shoestring.

The *El Tiempo* newspaper and the Cycling Assocation kept their end of the bargain and in an astonishingly short time, the race was organised.

On 5th January, 1951, 35 hardy souls – including of course Efraín Forero – were waved off from Bogotá by the editor of *El Tiempo*.

The first Vuelta was 1,157 kilometres long, divided into 10 stages with 2 rest days. The riders sweated in the tropical 35 degree heat of the lowlands and froze in the mountains. The descents on dirt roads were dangerous. The wheels and frames of their bikes – mostly locally fabricated – were not up to the stresses imposed on them by the rocks and the ruts in the roads.

Efraín Forero won the first stage, the descent from Bogotá to Honda, by twenty two minutes, despite six punctures. Close to the finish, he had to wade across the Rioseco River.

Jan 7, 1951. Efraín Forero climbing Letras, followed by his mother in the support truck.
*Foto José Betancur, El Colombiano*

Efraín Forero fording the Rioseco on his way to winning the first stage of the 1951 Vuelta
*Casa Editorial El Tiempo S.A.*

# 1951 Triumph of the indomitable Zipa

Efraín Forero wins the stage over Letras with "Jesse Owens" sprinting alongside him. Donald Raskin, the Englishman who masterminded the logistics of the event, holds the stopwatch on the finishing line.
*Casa Editorial El Tiempo S.A.*

The coverage in Colombia's newspapers reached stratospheric levels of excitement as the race progressed. According to *El Tiempo*, a crowd of seven thousand cheered Forero at the finish of the third stage in Manizales. His speed on the final descent was estimated at "close to a hundred kilometres per hour" and the running figure seen racing alongside Forero to the finish is confidently identified as "the well-known black runner, Jesse Owens." What the USA hero of the 1936 Olympics was doing in Colombia was not explained.

The blast of publicity was not confined to the newspapers. Colombia's radio stations covered the race, with broadcasts which started early in the morning and lasted most of the day. The commentators maintained fever pitch throughout, very different from the laconic style of Brian Smith and Sean Kelly on Eurosport today.

Efraín Forero's mother was in a support car behind her son but his father was back home in Zipaquira, along with a hundred of his neighbours, who clustered round the radio in his pharmacy from 7.30am until 4pm, listening to the commentators.

El Zipa did not disappoint his parents or the nation. Despite mechanical problems and the occasional crash, he won seven of the ten stages, including the final day from Girardot back to Bogota which he won by eight minutes. His overall lead was 2 hours and 20 minutes, an astonishing margin of victory which has never been repeated.

Bogota was in a frenzy.
El Tiempo, which had sponsored the race, estimated that 150,000 people turned out to greet the returning heroes. The police were unable to control the crowds, the city was paralysed and the riders were showered with gifts, large and small. The 'Millionaires' sporting club had a collection and presentation for the formidable Sara Triviño, Forero's mother. The "London tailor shop" offered a shirt of English cloth to the rider who came last. *El Tiempo* announced the *El Tiempo* trophy, made of silver, to be presented annually to the winner of the Vuelta.

EL TIEMPO

Apoteósis sin Precedentes rinde Bogotá a los Ciclistas

*Forero, Ganador de la Prueba Patrocinada por EL TIEMPO*

Ciento Cincuenta Mil Personas en el Grandioso Homenaje Deportivo

EL TIEMPO

Gran Movilización del Liberalismo en el Mes de Abril

Los Estudios para el Bachillerato Fueron Reformados Totalmente

Alza en el Precio de Carne Autorizó

Comunista Rechaza el Plan de Paz Presentado por la ONU

Habrá Nuevo Pacto Aéreo entre Colombia y los Estados Unidos

Loosely translated, the headline reads "Bogota treats the cyclists like gods"
*Casa Editorial El Tiempo S.A.*

Credit was widely shared.
The riders and their families, their sponsors, regions, the radio stations and newspapers, all congratulated each other and all were congratulated.
And so in just two weeks, the Vuelta a Colombia was created and the people of Colombia took her into their hearts.

Efraín Forero and his bride. *Ochoa family*

Promoted and feted by the social media of the day (the newspapers and the radio stations), cycling quickly became the national sport. A year later, for example, a "sportive" from Bogota to Facatativa and back attracted 1,135 amateur cyclists, including 25 from the national police. On the same day, there was an international meeting at Bogota's Velodrome featuring a world class field.

Colombia had fallen in love with cycling, and with the Vuelta a Colombia in particular.

# Efraín Forero Triviño

## Born
March 3rd, 1930
in Zipaquira,
Cundinamarca
Altitude: 2,632m

## Early days
Efraín Forero grew up in Zipaquira, a small town high up on the plateau of the eastern Andes, 60kms north of Bogota. Zipaquira is known for its salt mines and the underground Salt Cathedral, a church in a vast salt mine featuring the Stations of the Cross carved out of rock salt.

The young Forero got a job with the Soda plant in Zipaquira, which manufactured soda crystals and bicarbonate of soda from salt. It was an association which would last his whole life. His father ran a pharmacy. In 1948, when he was 18, some friends persuaded him to enter a local cycle race. The more experienced competitors made fun of his heavy touring bike and his football shorts. They did not laugh for long. "I said to myself, 'I will beat them or die'". Forero did not die; he won the race and went on to become the patriarch of Colombian road racing.

In 1949, he rode in the national cycling championship and in 1950, he represented Colombia in the Central American and Caribbean Games in Guatemala. His event was the 4km team pursuit. He and his fellow Colombians won gold, beating the Cubans into second place.

That year, he conceived the idea of a Colombian "Tour de France."

## Nickname
El Zipa Indomable
(the indomitable Zipa)

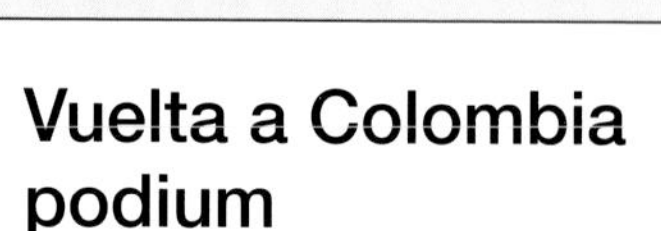

## Vuelta a Colombia podium
1951. Two other podium.

## Career
After founding the Vuelta and winning the first event by a wide margin, he became a national idol. Despite many attempts, he never won the Vuelta again.

## Vuelta a Colombia stages: 10

## Grand Tour & Other wins
None

## Later days
Eventually he gave up competing and became a team coach instead.

1952

# "Allons enfants de la patrie, le jour de gloire est arrivé!"

Argentine coaches Julio Arrastia and Roberto Guerrero: Antioquia's weapons in the search for revenge. *Biblioteca Publica Piloto, Medellin*

What did the second Vuelta have to do with the stirring words of the Marseillaise?

Colombia is a nation of competing departments, each with its own culture, tradition and geography. Efraín Forero was from Cundinamarca, a department which sprawls across the Eastern Cordillera, surrounding Bogota. Two hundred miles to the northwest lies the province of Antioquia, and its capital Medellin. Pedro Nel Gil, "the Tiger of Amalfi" and Roberto Cano, "the tailor of Envigado," who were runners up in the first Vuelta, were from Antioquia. Being soundly beaten by some fellow from Cundinamarca was a humiliating experience they did not wish to repeat. So with help from Donald Raskin, they hired two Argentine riders as coaches and began to train for the next encounter with El Zipa. The desire for revenge *by* or *over* the Antioqueños is a recurring theme in the history of Colombian cycling.

But it was not to be, at least not yet, *and certainly not as they intended*. Because in 1951, José Beyaert, the reigning Olympic road racing champion, arrived in Bogota to celebrate the opening on Bogota's new velodrome. He intended to stay for a month but was tempted by a sponsorship offer to ride in the 1952 Vuelta.

So Beyaert stayed on in the country and at 8am on 12th January, 1952, he lined up, along with last year's winner, Efraín Forero (el Zipa) and 58 others outside the offices of El Tiempo in Bogota. A crowd of 50,000 cheered them through the streets in person, and 16 radio stations, staffed by 41 broadcasters, kept the rest of the Colombian population informed.

José Beyaert did not enjoy his first encounter with Colombian road racing. He was shocked by the condition of the roads and confessed that he would have given up but his pride kept him going. At 2,640 metres (8,660 feet) above the sea, Bogota is one of the highest capitals in the world. Lowly Honda is 229 metres (751 feet) above the sea, so this first stage was a day of crazy fast descents on gravel and dirt.

There was general carnage. 19 riders were eliminated. There were multiple crashes.

José Beyaert, the Frenchman who won the 1952 Vuelta a Colombia, with his signature spectacles *Biblioteca Publica Piloto, Medellin*

The indomitable Zipa duelled all the way with an Argentine rider, Varisco, but finally lost out to him and came in six minutes behind. José Beyaert was 4th. Shocked as he was by the roads, the gradients and the general mayhem, the Frenchman Beyaert stuck to his guns and turned up the next day, ready to ride or die in the attempt.

Last to arrive in Honda was a 19 year old youth from Medellin called Ramón Hoyos (youth is relative: el Zipa was only 21 and Beyaert was 26). Hoyos had collided with a rock and was covered in blood. He had a 2 inch gash above his right eye, and the road had scraped the skin from his arms and back, but he had remounted his bike and pedalled on.

Original footage of riders on the perilous descent from Bogota to Honda (narrated by Efraín Forero).

An injured cyclist.
*BPP, Medellin*

1952

# "Allons enfants de la patrie, le jour de gloire est arrivé!"

By the time Hoyos got to the finish, the timekeeper and the crowds were gone, and he was disqualified. Hoyos was truly a novice. He had had a racing bike for all of two months. The El Tiempo journalist recalled going to see him in hospital:

*We remember the night we went, along with the doctor…to the bed where Ramón Hoyos lay. He looked more like a "civilian Christ" than a sportsman. He was covered in sticking plaster and bandages, his right eye almost closed, the surrounding flesh greenish, and his arms stiff as a board because of all the missing skin. The doctor examined him with speed and removed the bandages – without apology – to make a diagnosis. Hoyos made no sound and immediately got up to go to the surgery room of the hospital, just as the doctor ordered.*

Lying bandaged on his hospital bed, the battered youth surely feared that his race was over. However, the organizers – under pressure from the Army who had also had a rider disqualified – relented and reinstated 11 of those who had been disqualified the day before, including Ramón Hoyos. Unable to see out of his right eye, he nevertheless lined up at the start the next day.

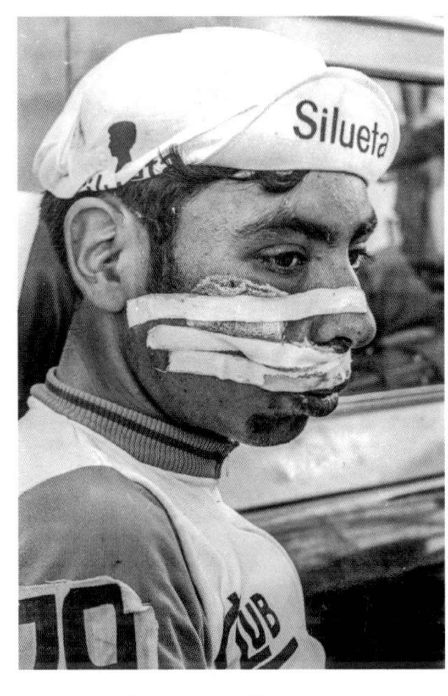


Hoyos must have looked like this young cyclist, bandaged and ready to ride again.
*Biblioteca Publica Piloto, Medellin*

The Frenchman Bayaert won the stage, a short one from Honda to Fresno. The indomitable Zipa, Efraín Forero, suffering from cramps and vomiting, came in 20 minutes behind.

The next day was a big one: the ride over the Alto de Letras to Manizales, which Forero had won in such style the year before. Urged on by his tireless mother from his support car, it looked as though he would do it again, but his luck deserted him. He had a heavy fall, and suffered severe grazing to his leg and elbow. At that moment, Beyaert launched a spirited attack, and disappeared into heavy fog on the mountain. He arrived at the top in the lead, closely followed – to the astonishment of onlookers – by young Ramón Hoyos. But Hoyos fell on the descent, leaving Beyaert to fly down, victorious, into Manizales.

A competitor ascending the Alto de Letras gets a friendly push... *Biblioteca Publica Piloto, Medellin*

Nevertheless, the no-hoper who had almost killed himself on the first stage was rapidly making a name for himself. El Tiempo's correspondent wrote:

*At Manizales, a new star rose in the heavens. What a great race from Ramón Hoyos, to come second ahead of Varisco, Forero Alberto Garcia and Cano Ramírez…despite having lost many hours in the first stage, today he is 16th in the GC!*

One interesting statistic: despite the fog and the rain, the top 15 finishers of this stage in 1952 all beat Forero's winning time of the year before. Colombian cyclists were learning the tactics of the peleton, how to avoid punctures, and perhaps – thanks to Donald Raskin's Argentine coaches – the importance of training.

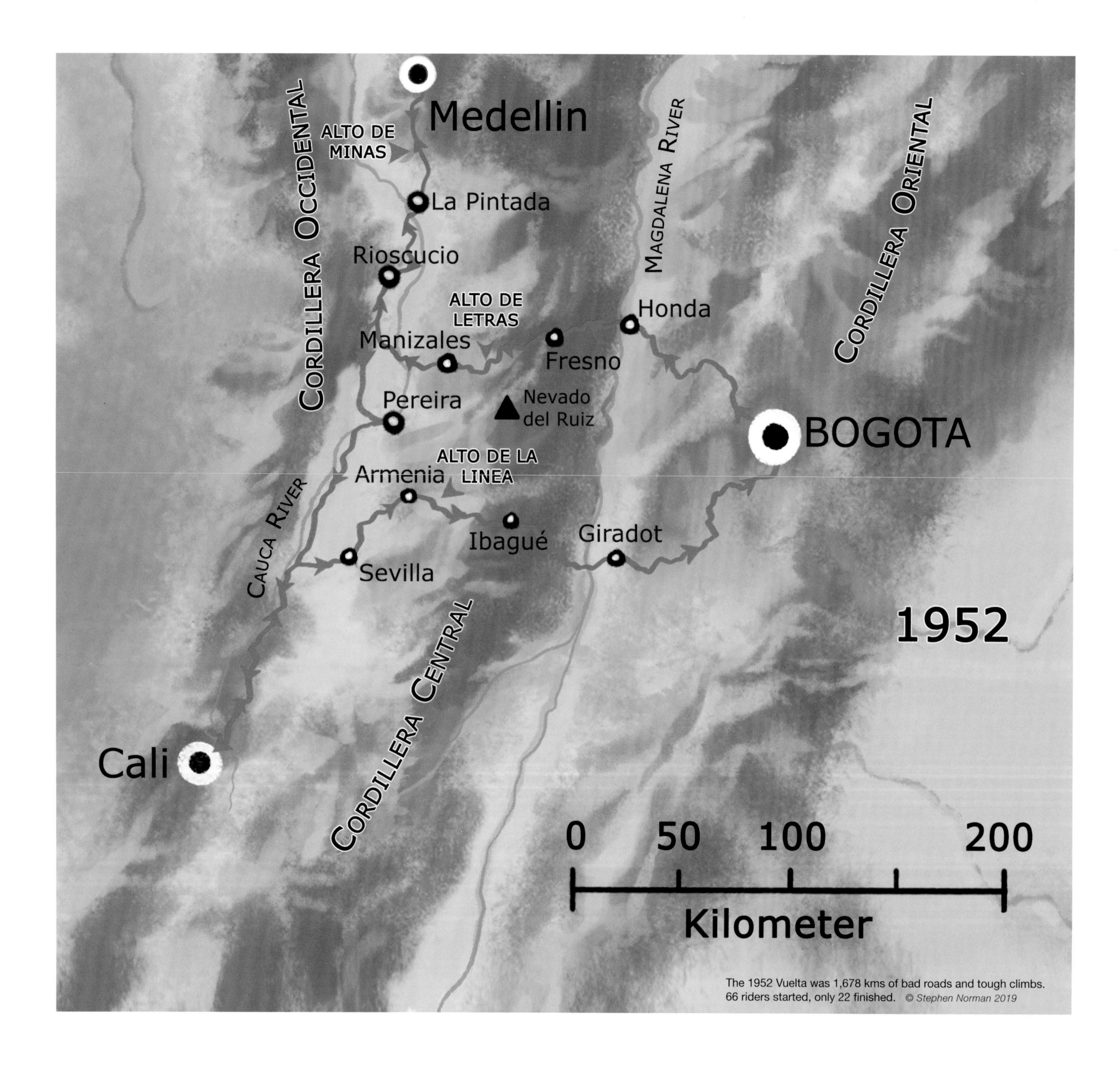
Medellin
ALTO DE MINAS
CORDILLERA OCCIDENTAL
MAGDALENA RIVER
CORDILLERA ORIENTAL
La Pintada
Rioscucio
ALTO DE LETRAS
Honda
Manizales
Fresno
Pereira
Nevado del Ruiz
BOGOTA
ALTO DE LA LINEA
Armenia
CAUCA RIVER
Ibagué
Giradot
Sevilla
1952
CORDILLERA CENTRAL
Cali
0
50
100
200
Kilometer
The 1952 Vuelta was 1,678 kms of bad roads and tough climbs.
66 riders started, only 22 finished.
© Stephen Norman 2019

1952

# "Allons enfants de la patrie, le jour de gloire est arrivé!"

The indomitable Zipa continued to be dogged by illness, mechanical problems and bad luck, but remained determined. Stage V was a brute, probably the toughest of the entire race. It had been added to the course since the previous year (see map).

It started at the little town of Riosucio. After 75 kilometres comprising 3 climbs of 500 metres and the difficult ascent to the town of Caramanta, the riders descended into the humid hothouse of the Rio Cauca valley. After crossing the river at La Pintada, they began the 42 kilometres ascent northward to the Alto de Minas, a climb of 2,000 metres, and descended to the finish in Medellin.

Forero, for once without mechanical problems, had led from the start. Hoyos was in 4th place, twenty minutes behind and José Beyaert in 8th place.

Incredibly, Hoyos, despite his injuries, made up the 20 minutes to the leader and caught La Zipa on the climb. They arrived at the top of the Alto de Minas together. It was the beginning of a bitter rivalry which was to last almost a decade.

On the descent, the Zipa's greater experience told. He cycled into the finish line in Medellin 4 minutes ahead of Hoyos, cheered on by a crowd of 100,000.

The race leader, José Beyaert, came in 33 minutes behind. El Zipa was now only 2 minutes behind the Frenchman in the General Classification. This is it, thought millions of Colombians, el Zipa's luck had changed. The foreigners were about to find out who were the real kings of the mountains.

Stage VI – after a rest day in Medellin – retraced the Stage V backwards, from Medellin over the Alto de Minas and down to Caramanta. Beyaert had a mechanical problem and El Zipa lent him one of his spare bikes.

Twenty minutes later, flying downhill from the Alto de Minas on a long straight, the front forks of Efraín Forero's bike sheared. Forero hit the road, still holding the handlebars. He took a violent blow to the head, just above his right eye.

With so many accidents and bad roads, the mechanics were busy half the night. fixing the bikes.
*Biblioteca Publica Piloto, Medellin*

# Foreigners can't win

There have been foreign riders in the Vuelta almost every year since 1952 but only five of them have ever won it. After Beyaert, the Spaniard José Gómez del Moral won in 1957. After that, there were 51 uninterrupted years of Colombian victories, until the Venezuelan José Rujano triumphed in 2009, to be followed by the Spaniard Oscar Sevilla, who won three years in a row.

José Gómez del Moral, a Spanish rider, won the 1957 Vuelta. It was 51 years before the next foreign victory, in 2009.
*Biblioteca Publica Piloto, Medellin*

# Climbing beetles of Colombia

Colombian cyclists are popularly known as "escarabajos". An escarabajo – a scarab – is a species of beetle, common in Colombia.

It was Ramón Hoyos was first called "un escarabajo", after his spectacular performance climbing the Alto de Letras in the 1952 Vuelta. It's not clear why. According to one version, an El Tiempo journalist got flustered on the radio. He meant to say that Hoyos "looked like a grasshopper on a bike," but the word "beetle" came out instead. Another version says that the commentator Carlos Arturo Rueda coined the name, because Hoyos climbed the Alto de Letras at such speed.

Whatever the truth, it wasn't long before every Colombian climber was proud to be called "an escarabajo."

# 1952

COLOMBIA FALLS IN LOVE

## "Allons enfants de la patrie, le jour de gloire est arrivé!"

Bleeding profusely, and in great pain, he accepted first aid from an army jeep. He tried to ride on, but it was too much, even for the Indomitable Zipa.
Beyaert – still on one of Forero's bikes – stopped to console him, then cycled on to win the stage. Young Hoyos was 6th, neck and neck with another young rider, famous for his descending skills, Tito Gallo.

El Zipa was forced to abandon the race and the country was inconsolable. The newspapers and the radio broadcasters were in shock, Miss Colombia sent him a personal message of support and three well placed Colombian riders vowed that they would win the Vuelta in homage to their hero. But at the end of Stage 7, José Beyaert was 14 minutes ahead!

On Stage 8, arriving in Cali, the leading four riders arrived at the line together in a photographic finish and recorded the same time. Beyaert still led by 14 minutes from the Argentine Varisco.

On the 9th stage, the upstart Ramón Hoyos put the rest of the cycling world on notice.
He won the stage by 15 seconds and Varisco took 6 minutes off Beyaert's lead.

The rest of the race became a duel between the Frenchman and the Argentine. On the penultimate stage, Varisco took another 12 minutes off Beyaert's lead. It was not enough! Beyaert stormed home on the last day, winning the stage by 90 seconds and the Vuelta by the tidy margin of 6 minutes. Ramón Hoyos finished sixth, beating his rival Tito Gallo by 18 minutes.

Efraín Forero was not the only rider to crash out of the 1952 Vuelta. The dreadful state of the roads and the difficulty of the route, which was 3 stages and 437 kilometres longer than the first year, led to wholesale attrition. In the first, 1951, Vuelta, 35 riders started – and 30 of them finished. In the 1952 Vuelta, 60 started and only 22 cycled into the new velodrome of Bogota on 27th January!

Crowds greet the riders arriving at the stadium in Medellin.
*Biblioteca Publica Piloto, Medellin*

Peleton passes over a mountain stream
*Biblioteca Publica Piloto, Medellin*

Ramón Hoyos, typically unsmiling.
*Biblioteca Publica Piloto, Medellin*

# 1953 The Antioquians fight back with Arrastia

Julio Arrastia treating Ramón Hoyos, probably for cramp. *Photo: José Betancur Yali*

In 1952, Olympic champion José Beyaert had proved himself the strongest, winning the last stage and the Vuelta outright. That was bad enough, but to add injury to insult, the runner up was another foreigner, the Argentine Varisco. The Colombians were gracious in defeat, but plotted revenge.

Especially the Antioquians, who went home to redouble their efforts with their Argentine coaching team. The lead man was Julio Arrastia, who turned out to be just the man for the job. Under his tutelage, the Antioquians became professionals. Training, equipment, and support were all industrialised for the first time.

Arrastia had seen Ramón Hoyos in action in the '52 Vuelta and liked what he saw. Hoyos was an ideal pupil. He was brutally ambitious, fearless and possessed of great technical skill.

In addition to his technical knowledge, Arrastia tempered determination with empathy. His riders loved him like a father.

His nickname 'El Viejo Macanudo,' Argentine slang meaning something like "what a great guy," reflected the affection that his pupils and colleagues felt for him.

Arrastia gave up as coach in 1959 and went on to be a radio commentator. He covered the Vuelta a Colombia 38 times between 1960 and his final retirement in 2005. Unsurprisingly, he soon earned a new nickname: "the Bible of Cycling."

The photographer Horacio Gil Ochoa described him poetically if enigmatically: "[He's] a bicycle, a race horse, a microphone, and a family. This man helped Colombian cycling for a long time. As a coach, as a teacher, and as a radio commentator, he was supreme, he just sat in his chair and he created a style."

Julio Arrastia: his riders loved him like a father.
*Biblioteca Publica Piloto, Medellin*

Professional training: Ricardo Zea watches Luis H Diaz on a roller trainer.
*Biblioteca Publica Piloto, Medellin*

Efraín Forero and his team over in Cundinamarca had also observed the foreigners at work, and recognised the benefits of their more rigorous approach. They didn't have a fancy foreign coach, but they were also training hard.

Everyone, in fact, was getting faster, as the next year was to prove.

# Ramón Hoyos Vallejo

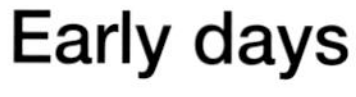

## Born
25th May, 1932
in Marinilla,
Antioquia
Altitude: 2,120m

## Nickname
Don Ramón de Marinilla

## Early days
He started riding when he was 12, on bikes from the local bike rental shop in Marinilla, near Medellin. Hoyos was sponsored by Ramiro Mejia, the owner of the Tropical Dry-Cleaner business. In 1951, Hoyos had won a circuit race in Manizales. His sponsor persuaded the organisers to let him race on a Monark touring bike, and later helped him get a place in the 1952 Vuelta. After his success in the 1952 Vuelta, he was able to buy a proper racing bike, an Automoto.

## Career
As well as his five GC wins of the Vuelta a Colombia, Hoyos competed in two Olympics in 1956 in Melbourne and 1960 in Rome. But he never broke into the international cycling stage.

## Later days
He opened a bike shop in Medellin in 1959 selling his own brand of bikes and curiously, he became a "radio ham", an amateur radio enthusiast.
Such was his standing in the country that Fernando Botero made a huge painting of him called the Apotheosis of Ramón Hoyos and Gabriel Garcia Marquez wrote a series of 14 articles based on interviews with him which were later published as a book.
His mother died in a huge landslide in July 12, 1954, in the suburb of Medio Luna, east of Medellin.

## Grand Tour & Other wins
He won the road race in the 1955 Pan American games in Mexico.

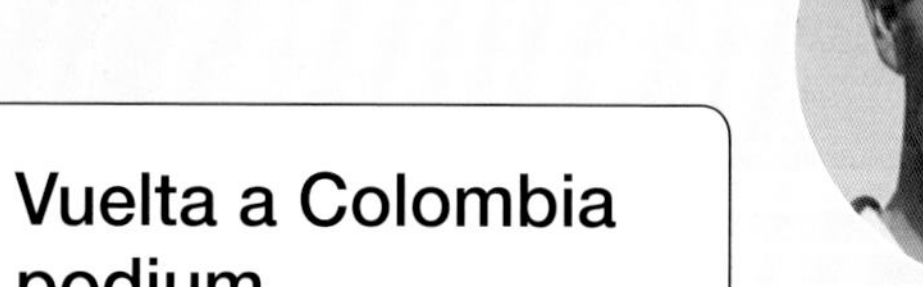

## Vuelta a Colombia podium
GC winner in 1953, 1954, 1955, 1957, 1958

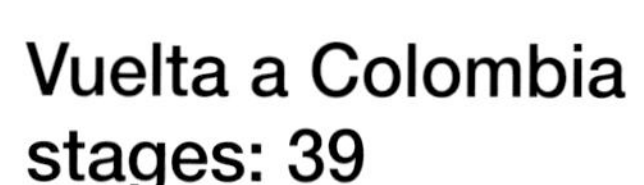

## Vuelta a Colombia stages: 39

# 1953 A new power arises in the West

The 1953 Vuelta started well for el Zipa. He won the first stage, setting a new record for the route from Bogota to Honda. "The Zipa is still indomitable!" screamed the newspapers.

The second short stage was won by an outsider, Carlos Orejuela, a rider from Huila, an Andean province southwest of Bogota, but only after a fierce duel with Ramón Hoyos, who crashed and lost a lot of time. Hoyos finished third, carrying the remains of his bike over the finishing line. The Zipa, who had suffered a puncture, came 4th.

The next day was the gruelling climb over the Alto de Letras. It was won by the Frenchman José Beyaert, who was back, riding with his brother Jorge.

And then, like the tide, the new order swept in.

Stage 5 ran from Riosucio to Medellin over the Alto de Minas, and the 6th stage returned in the opposite direction. El Tiempo, sponsor of the race, christened this route "169 kilometres of Death."

It was absolutely unsporting and wild. The descent to Supia, for example, was so challenging that even a great technician like Hoyos could not control his bike. When Hoyos fell, claimed El Tiempo, he screamed hysterically that he couldn't win and was going to give up.

Hoyos did not give up. He won both stages, and went on to win the next one, overtaking José Beyaert in the final kilometre leading into the finish at Pereira.

The Zipa, for all his preparation, did not have the team around him to shelter him or to lend him a bike when he punctured. Despite his constant challenges to Hoyos and the Antioquian team, he continued to lose time. Hoyos was greeted by ecstatic crowds in his native Medellin. Although he was on course for a stunning victory, aged twenty, photos of him show only the same stern face.

To be competitive in the Vuelta a team needed lots of bikes and swift changes.
*Biblioteca Publica Piloto, Medellin*

Ramón Hoyos might have passed this family on his triumphant ascent to Bogota. Horacio Gil Ochoa wrote on the back of this photo: *"Boyacá folk love cycling." Biblioteca Publica Piloto, Medellin*

And his victories continued. He began the last stage, the long climb up to the Andean plateau and Bogota, with an overall lead of 70 minutes. He didn't need to win, he just needed to finish.

But in fact Hoyos led the peleton almost from the start. 70 kilometres from Bogota, he turned on the power and accelerated away from the rest. He passed, solo, through the little towns before the capital, and entered Bogota. He crossed the finish line in the Bogota velodrome, cheered on by 30,000 Colombians. It was his 8th stage win. His overall margin of victory over the runner up, José Beyaert, was an astonishing 76 minutes.

Antioquian persistence and hard work with their Argentine coaches – as well as Arrastia's selection of Hoyos – had paid off. Antioquia was to remain King of the Cycling stakes for the rest of the '50s.

# The life and times of Ricardo Zea

Ramón Hoyos and Ricardo Zea in perfect harmony
*Biblioteca Publica Piloto, Medellin*

Ricardo Zea and Ramón Hoyos near Bogota. Date unknown. *BPP, Medellin*

Once a coach, always a coach! Ricardo Zea encourages two little girls at a Medellin party. *Biblioteca Publica Piloto, Medellin*

When Julio Arrastia moved from coaching to commentary, Ramón Hoyos needed a new coach, and he chose Ricardo Zea. Zea had many of the same qualities as Arrastia: he was dedicated, insightful and his riders loved him.

He and Hoyos developed a deep bond. They were in the words of a Colombian proverb, inseparable like "fingernail and grime."

In the picture below it is Hoyos who is covered in blood, but as Ochoa remarked "they are both suffering."

During the 60s, Ricardo Zea became a close friend of Roberto Escobar, brother of Pablo. And after he retired from the cycling world, he got a job as a manager on the Escobars' estate.

Being close to the Escobars became dangerous as their criminal empire collapsed during the 1990s. In 1993 he was murdered by Los Pepes, the vigilante group that made war on Pablo's associates and property.

# 1954-1955 A new power arises in the West

Hoyos and the Antioquian team - lean and mean.
*Biblioteca Publica Piloto, Medellin*

In 1954, Hoyos won Vuelta a Colombia again, this time by 47 minutes (a modest margin, for him). The adoring Colombian public showered him with so many gifts and prizes from his stage wins that the Army had to provide a separate truck to carry them.

Six months later, his beloved mother and sister were killed in a landslide, along with 73 others, which engulfed a suburb of Medellin. He described to the writer and journalist Gabriel Garcia Marquez how he passed through the spot on a race, and how he stopped to pray two hail marys. "When I returned to the race, I was no longer in the lead but 6th or 7th. So I pedalled hard and as I did, I spoke to my mother in heaven, and she helped me."

By 1955, the race attracted more foreign riders. Not just Beyaert, who had made his home in Colombia, but teams from Argentina, Venezuela and Mexico.

The foreigners might as well have stayed at home. Hoyos' dominance was total. He won the first six stages in a row, establishing a substantial lead. He never lost it and went on to win 12 stages in total. Hoyos won the 1955 Vuelta by 90 minutes.

In the same year, Hoyos went to the Pan American games in Mexico and won both the road race as an individual, and the team trial. After winning the race, he was hoisted aloft by delirious Mexican admirers. In the fracas, someone stole his cycling shoes. "I see they cook beans everywhere," he remarked dryly, returning barefoot to his hotel.

# Hernán Medina Calderón

## Born
29th August,1937
in Yarumal,
Antioquia
Altitude 2,265m

## Nickname
The Student Prince

## Early days
His parents insisted that he study – everything else comes after the homework. Julio Arrastia, the Argentine coach of the Antioquian team, saw him riding around outside his high school and insisted that he ride.

## Career
After his extraordinary leap into the lead of the 1957 Vuelta – and subsequent disappointment when his team withdrew – he was second in 1958 (and King of the Mountain) and won the Tour of Guatamala that year. He was second again in 1959 and he finally won the Vuelta in 1960. That year also he was King of the Mountain in the Tour of Mexico. In 1961 he was second again, to Rubén Darío Gómez.

## Later days
The student prince got off his bike in El Campin stadium at the finish of the 1961 Vuelta and went to college to study Mechanical Engineering.
He would not compete again. For fifteen years, he worked at Antioquia's premium beer company, Cervecería Unión. Later he founded his own transport business and worked in that for 28 years. Now retired, he still enjoys cycling and has ridden the routes of the Tour de France as a tourist.

## Vuelta a Colombia podium
1960 (but 2nd in 1958, 1959, 1961)

## Vuelta a Colombia Stages: 9

## Grand Tour & Other wins
None

# 1957 Year of the Student Prince

Hoyos had won each Vuelta a Colombia from 1953 to 1956, and everyone expected him to make it five in a row in 1957.

But the Vuelta had a surprise for them. On June 27, 1957, a young unknown led the pack into the main square of Riosucio, completing the dangerous descent from Medellin over the Alto de Minas. His nearest rival was three minutes behind. El Zipa didn't arrive for another 20 minutes, and Ramón Hoyos (who was fighting a stomach infection) for half an hour!

The newcomer not only won the stage, but now led the General Classification by 14 minutes. It was an amazing achievement for someone riding in his first Vuelta. His name was Hernán Medina and he was nineteen years old.

Many of the great Colombian riders came from rural backgrounds, high in the mountains, and left school early to work for a living. Not Hernán Medina Calderón. He was a chemistry student at the University of Antioquia, and cycled in his spare time. Recognising his extraordinary talent, the Union Brewery had sponsored him for the 1957 Vuelta.

The radio commentator Carlos Rueda – following him up the Alto de la Linea in the 1958 Vuelta – nicknamed him "the Student Prince," and the name stuck.

At that moment, in the main square of Riosucio, the Student Prince looked favourite to win the race outright, especially since Ramón Hoyos was so clearly ill. Hoyos had come in 18th on this stage – 30 minutes behind Medina – and announced that he was on the point of quitting.

But politics intervened. The race judges said that Hoyos had been pushed on the climb to the Alto de Minas that day, and penalised him 5 minutes. Indignant, the entire Antioquian team including young Hernán Medina was withdrawn from the race. The Vuelta was won by a Spaniard.

It was a heartbreaking moment for the Student Prince.

Hernán Medina, the Student Prince, feeling the pain *Biblioteca Publica Piloto, Medellin*

# "You've just beaten the best cyclist in the world"

Fausto Coppi and Hugo Koblet were defeated by the brutal conditions in the Doble a Pintada, 1958
*Biblioteca Publica Piloto, Medellin*

The year 1958 started well for Ramón Hoyos. One of the greatest cyclists who ever lived, the Italian Fausto Coppi and his friend Hugo Koblet were visiting Colombia and the organisers had put on a series of races to entertain the public.

1958. Colombian TV news clip shows Coppi racing in the velodrome, prior to his crushing defeat by Ramón Hoyos on the Alto de Minas.

The climax was "the Doble a Pintada," meaning "the race to Pintada and back." This route from Medellin over the Alto de Minas to La Pintada was the one the journalists had christened "the stage of death," on account of the numerous accidents that had taken place on the 42 kilometres descent from the Alto de Minas.

There were no accidents on the descent for Coppi, Koblet and their Colombian hosts. Koblet reached La Pintada first. It was unbearably hot down by the river.

After an hour's rest, the riders returned in the timed order in which they arrived. Hoyos went after Koblet, followed by the precocious Student Prince, Hernán Medina.

Emociones, Dolores y Triunfos del Ciclismo

FOTOS DE MAZ y BETANCUR para EL COLOMBIANO

Photo coverage of the 1958 defeat of Coppi and Koblet in El Colombiano the next day. Bottom left shows Hugo Koblet slumped over his handlebars after being overtaken by Ramón Hoyos. In the centre he is being helped into an ambulance by two assistants. *El Colombiano*

42 kilometres down, means 42 agonising kilometres back up to the Alto de Minas. Koblet cracked first, abandoning the race. Hoyos passed him, then overtook Coppi, and so did Medina.

## *A curious footnote:*

*Watching the destruction of Coppi and Koblet that day was an eight year old boy, who had been ferried up the hill from Medellin on the handlebars of his older brother's bike. The boy was Pablo Escobar, and his brother was Roberto Escobar, later to become a successful Colombian cyclist, founder of a cycling team and the Ositto bicycle brand. And in later years, a narco-trafficker alongside Pablo.*

Finally, Coppi collapsed on the side of the road.

The defeat of this great cyclist – although he was 38 years old and not at the peak of his powers – made headlines around the world. It confirmed to Colombians the godly nature of their own cyclists, and especially Don Ramón Hoyos.

# 1958 Return of the King

After racing together in Colombia, Hoyos and el Zipa went with the great Italian champion Fausto Coppi and his friend Hugo Koblet on a trip to Mexico, to take part in a series of exhibition races there.

Alas, the organiser ran out of funds. There were no events. Hoyos wound up penniless in Mexico City, without even the price of a ticket home.

Eventually he made it home in time to start the 1958 Vuelta.

Fuelled by righteous anger, he regained his crown from the young upstart Medina, who came second. It was his last win and the end of an era.

Ramón Hoyos out in front near Tunja 1958. *"Even the champion's shorts have been lacerated by his power," wrote Ochoa on the back.* Biblioteca Publica Piloto, Medellin

What? Still not at the top? Ramón Hoyos grinding up a big climb. Note the huge bruise on his cheek. *Biblioteca Publica Piloto, Medellin*

# Rubén Darío Gómez

## Born
3rd March,1940
in Santa Rosa de Cabal, Risaralda
Altitude 1,691m

## Nickname
El Tigrillo de Pereira
(the Little Tiger of Pereira)

## Vuelta a Colombia podium
1959, 1961 with 6 podium places (1960 3rd,1963 2nd, 1964 2nd, 1965 3rd)

## Vuelta a Colombia stages: 16

## Grand Tour & Other wins
RCN Clásico (1961, 1962)

## Early days
He was third in a family of 12 children. His father was a carpenter and painter in Pereira. He started cycling in secret because his father forbade him to race. Despite winning the novice prize in the Vuelta, aged 18, in 1958, he had no money to race in the 1959 Vuelta, until a local priest organised a parade round Pereira in an old car with a basket for food and money. Rubén Darío Gómez and his team won the Vuelta that year. It was an extraordinary victory for a team from Pereira against the might of Antioquia. In gratitude, the citizens of Pereira gave each of the 4 riders a plot to build a house in the city, and volunteers to build them.

## Later days
After hanging up his bike, he became a coach and helped Rafael Antionio Niño to his Vuelta victory in 1973, and afterwards he coached the national team in Europe in 1983 and 1984.

## Career
Rubén Darío Gómez won the Vuelta twice and the Clásico RCN twice, and probably would won more had he not come up against Martín Emilio Cochise Rodríguez! He competed in 13 Vueltas, and rode for Colombia in the Olympic Games in Rome (1960) and Tokyo (1964). He was one of the "Pereira Four" who challenged the supremacy of Antioquia in the 1960s. They were Pablo Hernandez, Rubén Darío Gómez, Alfonso Galvis and Ariel Betancurt.

# 1959 Joy in Pereira

Ruben Dario Gomez pursued by Antioquians. Hernan Medina (left), Ramon Hoyos (centre).
*Copyright: El Tiempo, 6th June 1959*

The 1959 Vuelta was won by a brilliant newcomer, Ruben Dario Gomez. He was barely 19 years old when he crossed the line in Bogota. He remains to this day the youngest winner in the history of the Vuelta.

Gomez was an outsider. He came from Pereira, in the department of Risaralda, south of Medellin. Risaralda was smaller and less important than Antioquia or Boyaca. He had no professional coaching. He was the 3rd child of a family of 12. His father was an intermittently employed painter and decorator. He had to train in secret because his father had forbidden him to race.

The newspaper cutting above shows Gomez (in front) leaving Honda on the last day, surrounded by men from Medellin: Medina on the left, then Hoyos, a pack of Antioquians, all hungry for the kill. To the everlasting delight of Pereira, he stayed ahead all the way to Bogota.

The Student Prince must have felt that the gods were against him, again! He finished second and Hoyos was fourth.

Local girls admire the race leader climbing out of town. *Biblioteca Publica Piloto, Medellin*

Even the mule is captivated! Luis A Munoz in action in the 1959 Vuelta.
*Biblioteca Publica Piloto, Medellin*

Taking the chequered flag: Hernán Medina came from nowhere and might have won the 1957 Vuelta a Colombia if politics had not intervened.
*Biblioteca Publica Piloto, Medellin*

# 1960 Student Prince crowned at last

In 1960, the Student Prince finally achieved the victory which politics had snatched away from him in 1957. It was a close run thing. He was defending second place most of the way round, with Hoyos breathing down his neck. On the penultimate day, after an enormous battle, he won the stage and took the leader's tricolour jersey.

The race finished with another brutal climb over Minas, from Riosucio to Medellin. Pursued all the way by Hoyos and another young talent, Roberto Buitrago, Medina battled on, coming in second but retaining his overall lead. The Vuelta was his! Ramón Hoyos was fourth and announced that this had been his last Vuelta.

With Hoyos out of the picture, the youngsters – Hernán Medina, Rubén Darío Gómez and Roberto Buitrago must have felt that 'tomorrow belonged to them'. It did, but only briefly. For as Hoyos left the stage, another giant was waiting in the wings.

Water-cooled Roberto Buitrago. Notice the label "La Jaula," – the cage – on the truck carrying Buitrago's brothers. So they were the birds in the cage and he was el Pajarito, "the little bird."
*Biblioteca Publica Piloto, Medellin*

The state of the roads took a heavy toll on the machines. Here, mechanics work long into the night to repair wheels and tyres for the next day.
*Biblioteca Publica Piloto, Medellin*

Cactus watching the peleton go by. *BPP, Medellin*

# Desperation of youth

1. The rider in black shorts has had a mechanical problem or a puncture. Desperate not to lose time, he leaves the bike and starts running up the road.

*Biblioteca Publica Piloto, Medellin*

2.The bike is fixed. His mechanic rides after him.

*Biblioteca Publica Piloto, Medellin*

3. He sees the bike coming.

*Biblioteca Publica Piloto, Medellin*

4. Jumps back on...

*Biblioteca Publica Piloto, Medellin*

5. ... rides off. Phew!

*Biblioteca Publica Piloto, Medellin*

# 1961-1969 COCHISE, COCHISE, COCHISE

## 1961 Martín Emilio Rodríguez

Martín Emilio Rodriquez on a touring bike wins his first race (note the chequered flag at the top of the picture). His eyes are wide open and fixed on the camera – or is it the future? *Photo: Ochoa family but photographer unknown*

Martín Emilio Rodríguez was just 18 years old when he joined the riders at the start of the 1961 Vuelta. He had every reason to feel nervous. He was surrounded by prodigious and experienced talent, including Hernán Medina, Rubén Darío Gómez, Roberto Buitrago and the venerable presence of el Zipa himself, Efraín Forero.

It didn't seem to bother him. The classic Colombian cyclist is a climber, light and skinny with big lungs and great power to weight ratio. Cochise – as he came to be known – was cast in a different mould. He was of medium build but physically very strong. He combined the physique of a sprinter with the endurance of a climber.

The strength of this combination became apparent on the third stage. While they were in the mountains, Cochise duelled for the leadership position with two previous winners, Hernán Medina and Rubén Darío Gómez. But the finish was on the flat. Cochise turned on the power, and beat both his rivals in the sprint for the line. Aged 18, he had just won a stage in the Vuelta a Colombia. When the '61 Vuelta finished in the stadium in Bogota, he was in 6th place overall, an hour ahead of el Zipa.

1961 was a year of triple triumph for Rubén Darío Gómez and the team from Pereira. They took the team trophy, and Gómez won General Classification and the King of the Mountains.

For the Antioquians, Hernán Medina was second, yet again. He was 23 years old. He had ridden in five Vueltas, won one and finished on the podium four times.

He was a young man with a plan for his life. He got off his bike and went off to college to study Mechanical Engineering. He never cycled again competitively.

Mechanics repair and reflate spare wheels on the move. *Biblioteca Publica Piloto, Medellin*

Now preparing to swap bikes... *BPP, Medellin*

The father of Colombian cycling, Efraín Forero, also retired for the last time in 1961. He had previously quit in 1959, because he needed to work to pay off the debts he had accumulated while cycling.

The young Cochise powers to the finish in Cali. He is about to win his first stage.
The photographer Horacio Gil called this "his favourite photograph".
*Biblioteca Publica Piloto, Medellin*

Efraín Forero tells the story of his cycling career.

# Antioquia

Every department of Colombia has its own regional characteristics, but none so consciously distinctive as Antioquia. Antioquians wear different clothes, have a distinct accent and their own distinctive cuisine. They call themselves "paisas", or "country folks." Antioquians feel superior to their fellow citizens in Bogota or elsewhere who sit on the Cordillera Oriental. And their capital, Medellin, is a vibrant modern city with a lot going for it, except the traffic and the queues to buy subway tickets.

Medellin has a strong artistic and musical tradition. The centre of Medellin is liberally sprinkled with the giant, exuberant sculptures of Fernando Botero, who lived here and who donated his work to the city. The galleries are full of his paintings.

Parade of silleteros in Medellin *Photo El Colombiano*

A Botero sleeping nude (Medellin) *Photo Stephen Norman*

Medellin is surrounded by flower farms, and the city hosts a magnificent flower festival each year, including a parade of silliteros – flower growers – carrying wooden frames on their backs which hold rich flower displays.

Antioquia is big on farming. In the cold highlands on the Occidental and Central cordilleras, they grow potatoes, wheat and barley. Down in the hot, humid valleys of the Magdalena and Cauca rivers, they grow rice, maize and plantains. But in-between, they grow coffee and sugar cane, which they export. And a lot of beef.

When paisas dine, they dine off a "paisa platter," which is a plate laden with food. This incredible spread includes a little – no, a lot – of everything. Fried pork, hogao onion jam, beef, chorizo, plantains, rice, all rounded off with a fried egg on top. And of course arepas, a kind of cheesy flatbread that every Antioquian will snack on whenever they get peckish.

next left page

Fredonia, a short ride from Medellin *Photo Cyclota.com*

# 1962 The battle of the five teams

Roberto Buitrago leads Rubén Darío Gómez out of Anserma in the 1962 Vuelta a Colombia
*Biblioteca Publica Piloto, Medellin*

After a year of coaching, Cochise was back.

The 1962 was one of the most thrilling Vueltas of all time. It was closely fought every inch of the way to the line in Bogota.

At the end of the first stage, 6 cms separated first and second place. The peleton, Cochise among them, were less than 2 minutes behind. Rubén Darío Gómez was on form, but there were new Antioquians, not only Cochise but also a novice rider called Javier Suárez.

By the 4th stage, only 4 minutes divided the first 20 riders.

Cochise took the 5th stage after a long battle with a Spanish rider, and found himself just 26 seconds behind Rubén Darío Gómez.

But the 1962 Vuelta had plenty of surprises in store. Gómez had a bad day, and lost his place. Briefly the lead was held by a Spanish rider, and two other Colombians.

The 11th stage was the infamous Ride of Death, from Riosucio over the Alto de Minas to Medellin. It was won by a rider even less experienced than Cochise, Javier Suárez.

Javier Suárez was 18 years old. He had never won a race before.

His mother Rosa was herself a precocious mother – she was in her early teens when he was born, in a poor suburb of Medellin. Cochise was second, 4 minutes behind. It was enough to give Suárez the leader's tricolour jersey and Cochise remained in second place.

The next day was the stage from Medellin over the Alto de Minas. Suárez finished second to an experienced rider, Robert Buitrago, and held on to the leader's jersey, but faded the next day.

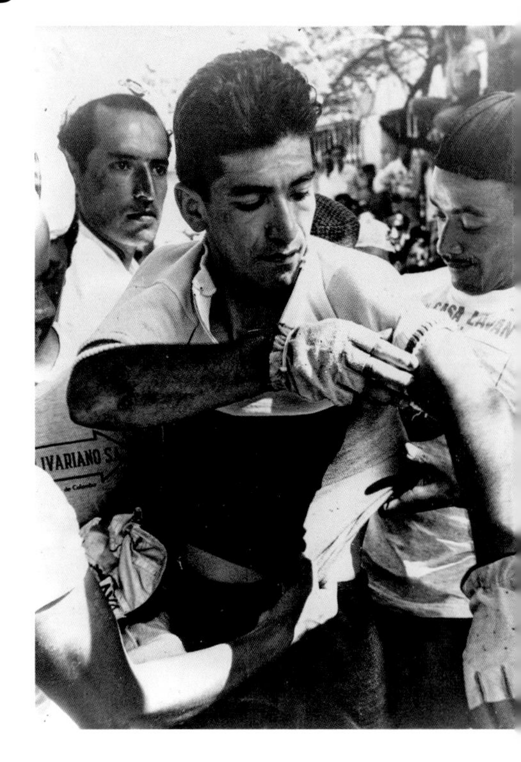

Pajarito Buitrago dons the leaders jersey in the epic 1962 Vuelta a Colombia
*Biblioteca Publica Piloto, Medellin*

Hoyos and Buitrago: friends and rivals
*Biblioteca Publica Piloto, Medellin*

# Antioquia

On your way from Bogota to Medellin you may ascend the mighty Alto de Letras and get this view, 70 kms up the climb.
*Photo Cyclota.com*

from previous left page

Of course they don't eat this every day, and in Medellin and the other cities of Antioquia, you can eat Chinese or tapas or whatever takes your fancy, and you can wash it down with a cappuccino that might have come straight from Milan.

Of course, Medellin is trying to forget. Forget that it was the city of Pablo Escobar and the Medellin cartel and the terrible violence that accompanied his final years. The word cocaine is taboo in Medellin. They have never heard of it.

Antioquia has great parks, both around the city, and elsewhere. Heading east from Medellin, you come to the colourful town of Guatape, with its lake and the huge rock overlooking it (740 steps up but incredi-ble views from the top). Or head out to the whitewashed colonial town of Jardin, and the coffee country. Or go bird-watching. Colombia is home to almost 20% of all the bird species on the planet.

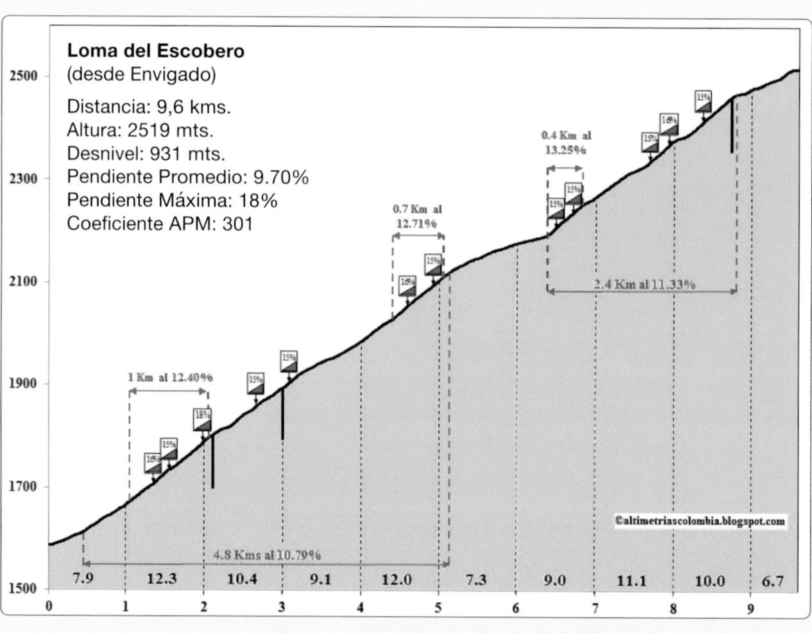


The Loma de Escobero is a short sharp climb out of Medellin.
*Altimetria www.altimetriascolombia.blogspot.com*

## *Cycling notes*

*Medellin lies in a deep valley and the hills rise to 3,000 metres on all sides. Which makes for great climbing. You can retrace Oscar Sevilla's close run victories in the Vuelta and cycle east out of town to the Loma del Escobero, or to the Alto de las Palmas. The Loma del Escobero is 9.6 kilometres long, and 931 metres of ascent, so you will deserve the great views from the top.*

*Or if you've got the support and the bike, try the Doble over the Alto de Minas to La Pintada...and back again. Just remember that Coppi and Koblet came back on the bus!*

Mayor of Medellin (left) with author (centre) and Jesus Chucho Piedrahita (right) at the finish of the Vuelta 2018.
*Photo Pamela Gowland*

# 1962 The battle of the five teams

Cochise remained strong. At the start of the final day, he was just 10 seconds down on Buitrago. Right from the start in La Dorada, he attacked constantly, and Buitrago and his teammates struck back. Neither succeeded.

And then, going down the Alto de Tigre, Buitrago had a puncture. "I could tell by the long faces of my companions that they thought it was all over," he said.

After 6 hours and 46 minutes on the road, Martín Emilio 'Cochise' Rodríguez had beaten Robert Buitrago by just 2 seconds. It was not enough, since he started the stage 10 seconds down. Cochise lost the 1962 Vuelta a Colombia by just 8 seconds.

50 years have not dimmed Buitrago's pleasure: "Winning was the greatest happiness of my life as a cyclist. To beat a paisa [an Antioquian] was the bestest! That rivalry was precisely what made the Vuelta a Colombia at that time. Today I still remember the stadium packed, chanting my name and I climbed on the shoulders of my supporters."

Cochise enters the stadium 20 metres ahead of Buitrago... *Biblioteca Publica Piloto, Medellin*

Roberto Buitrago winning a hilltop finish – date unknown. *Biblioteca Publica Piloto, Medellin*

Roberto Buitrago retired that year, and then got married the next. But in 1965, he weakened, and came back for a season. He was still good. He held the lead for a stage, and came 3rd in the King of the Mountains.

Gabriel Halaixt repairing a puncture
*Biblioteca Publica Piloto, Medellin*

Cochise loses the 1962 Vuelta by 8 seconds to Buitrago. *Biblioteca Publica Piloto, Medellin*

# The stage of death

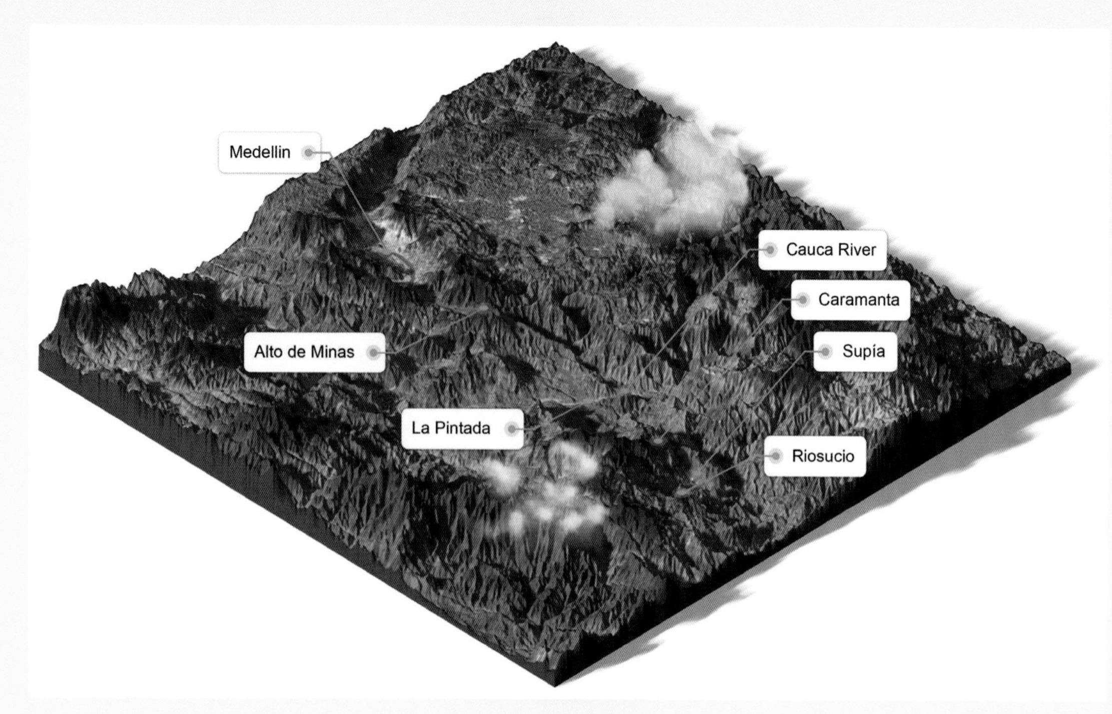


Riosucio to Medellin and its reverse. Two of the toughest and most dangerous stages of the Vuelta a Colombia
*© Stephen Norman*

The monster Alto de Letras and La Linea both cross the Central Cordillera. Traditionally the Vuelta, starting from Bogota, would cross one of them from east to west and come back by the other.

The 1952 Vuelta introduced an additional pair of mountainous stages: from Riosucio to Medellin, and back again.

Riosucio (literally "dirty river" in Spanish) is a town and municipality in the department of Caldas in Colombia. It is famous for its biennial carnival, commonly known as the "Carnival of the Devil".
It is one of the biggest and most popular carnivals in Colombia.

On leaving Riosucio, the route north to Medellin descends to Supia (1183 metres) and then climbs to the tiny hilltop town of Caramanta (2,050 metres) before descending to cross the river Cauca at La Pintada (647 metres).
At this point, the cyclist has covered 50 mountain miles. This is just the warm up. From the heat and flies of the river Cauca, the climb begins to the Alto de Minas, 42 kilometres away.

A recent blogger[18] described the climb:
*The Alto de Minas climb is more than 40 kilometres of complete torture. This brutal Colombian ascent has slopes of up to 11% in several sectors. It has been widely used in prestigious races such as the Vuelta a Colombia and Clásico RCN.*

*The difficulty of the climb is partly due to its length, 42 kilometres , but also the humidity and heat. In addition to the heavy traffic that regularly transits this way.*

*The difficult stretch begins when you get past La Quiebra, a natural bridge between two mountains, with delightful drops on both sides of the road. After that there is 8.1 kilometres of 7% of average slope, with the ravine always on the right. Halfway through the hard section we take a wide curve of the valley and from there to the town of Santa Bárbara we can see the winding road that we have ascended."*

next left page

Vuelta a Colombia 1953: Tito Gallo before his accident descending Alto de Minas. *Biblioteca Publica Piloto Medellin*

18 See Alto de Minas on alpsandes.com

# 1963 Coronation

Cochise returned a year later, determined to show who was king. He won the 3rd and 4th stages, but still lagged behind Rubén Darío Gómez.

Until the 6th stage, that is. The stage started in Medellin and ran over the Alto de Tigre (2,180 metres) and finished in Riosucio.

Cochise reached the summit in the lead. Javier Suárez was half a bike behind and the race leader Rubén Darío Gómez 3 minutes behind.

They were 20 kilometres from the finish in Riosucio.

Descending with awesome skill, Cochise destroyed the opposition on the descent to Riosucio. Suárez clung to his wheel but was dropped 10 kilometres later.

400 metres from the finish, Cochise had a puncture but did not stop. He crossed the line on bare metal rims. His GC lead over Rubén Darío Gómez was almost 5 minutes. It was the beginning of a triumphant parade.

He won 3 more stages, including the time trial, and retained the leader's jersey for 9 stages in succession. By the time he entered the stadium in Bogota, his lead was 33 minutes.

It was a performance worthy of Ramón Hoyos himself. A new national hero was born.

Vuelta a Colombia 1963: the race is held up! Riders, coaches, officials (see the timekeeper on the left with his stopwatches) wait patiently for the off. *Biblioteca Publica Piloto, Medellin*

Cochise, Suárez and Salazar share a hotel room on a rest day; traditionally the Vuelta had 2 rest days, one in Medellin. *BPP, Medellin*

# The stage of death

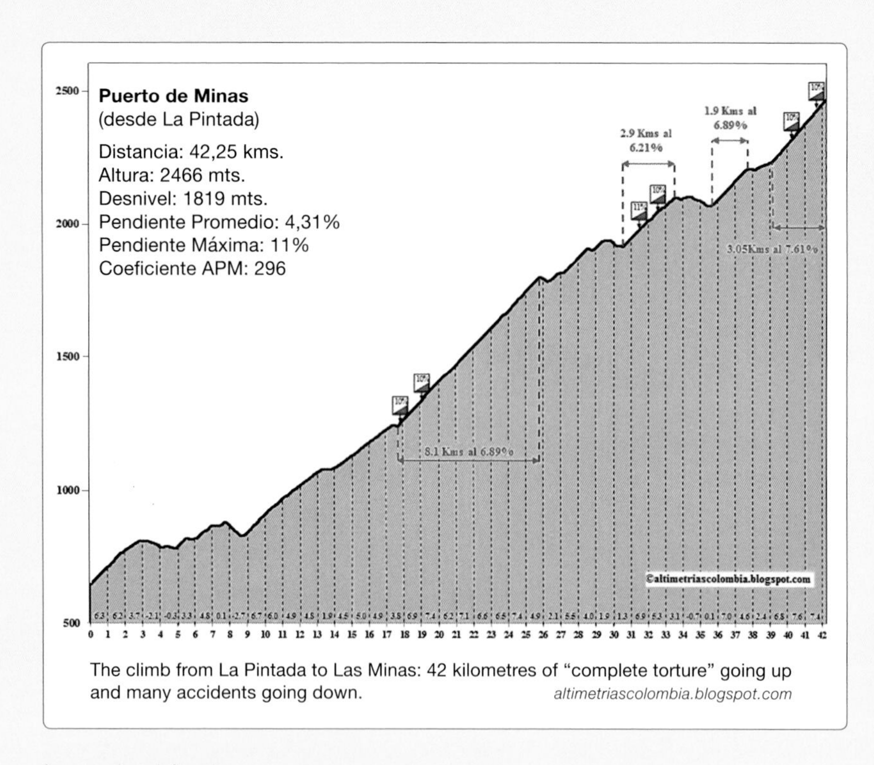


The climb from La Pintada to Las Minas: 42 kilometres of "complete torture" going up and many accidents going down. *altimetriascolombia.blogspot.com*

from previous left page

Having survived the 42 kilometres to the pass at Alto de Minas, there is a swift and sinuous descent into the town of Caldas, and then on to Medellin.

On many occasions, the Vuelta would rest a day in Medellin, perhaps combined with a time trial, and then take the route back over Minas to Riosucio. This tough stage has been the scene of many extraordinary triumphs and tragedies over the years.

It was on the ascent from La Pintada in 1952 that the precocious Hoyos caught up 20 minutes on the Zipa, and battled with him all the way down. The Zipa was quicker on the descent, and won the stage.

On the return, the Zipa flew down from Minas, leaving the rest behind. 8 kilometres from the bottom at La Pintada, his forks sheared. He suffered a severe blow above his eyebrow, and had to retire from the race.

The next year, 1953, Hoyos led the race over Las Minas, heading into Medellin. Behind him was the Frenchman Beyaert and an Antioquian teammate of Hoyos, Conrado 'Tito' Gallo.

Tito Gallo was a crazy descender of great skill. But his skill couldn't help him when – just like el Zipa the year before – his forks sheared, pitching him headfirst onto the road. He suffered severe head injuries. He was in a coma for seven weeks, close to death, and was mentally and physically impaired for the rest of his life.

It was on the ascent from La Pintada to the Alto de Minas in 1958 that Hoyos and then Hernán Medina overtook the great Italian rider Coppi and his friend Hugo Koblet. Both foreigners abandoned on that climb.

This victory over the legendary Coppi convinced Colombian enthusiasts that their boys were unbeatable.

In the 1982 Vuelta, the precocious 21 year old Lucho Herrera, who had just won the Clásico RCN, came over the top of the Alto de Minas, duelling with Fabio Parra. But Herrera had a bad fall on the descent and had to pull out of the race.

The funeral of Tito Gallo, many years after the accident which left him debilitated and unable to speak. *Photo Ospina*

1964

# The 1964 Vuelta was a monster.

The 1964 Vuelta was a monster. Like the Tour de France, it kicked off with the flat stages up in the North, and moved onto the mountains for the second half. The starting point was Santa Marta, on the Caribbean coast, and it finished in Bogota. In between there were 19 stages and 2,445 kilometres of hard road.

The nation was expectant and Cochise did not disappoint. He won the 200 kilometres third stage from the Caribbean city of Cartagena to Sincelejo, and became overall leader.

He retained the tricolour jersey for the rest of the Vuelta. He won 9 stages outright, including both time trials.

In case his rivals hadn't got the message, he won the final stage into the stadium in Bogota. He really didn't need to – he was already 1 hour and 30 minutes ahead of the competition!

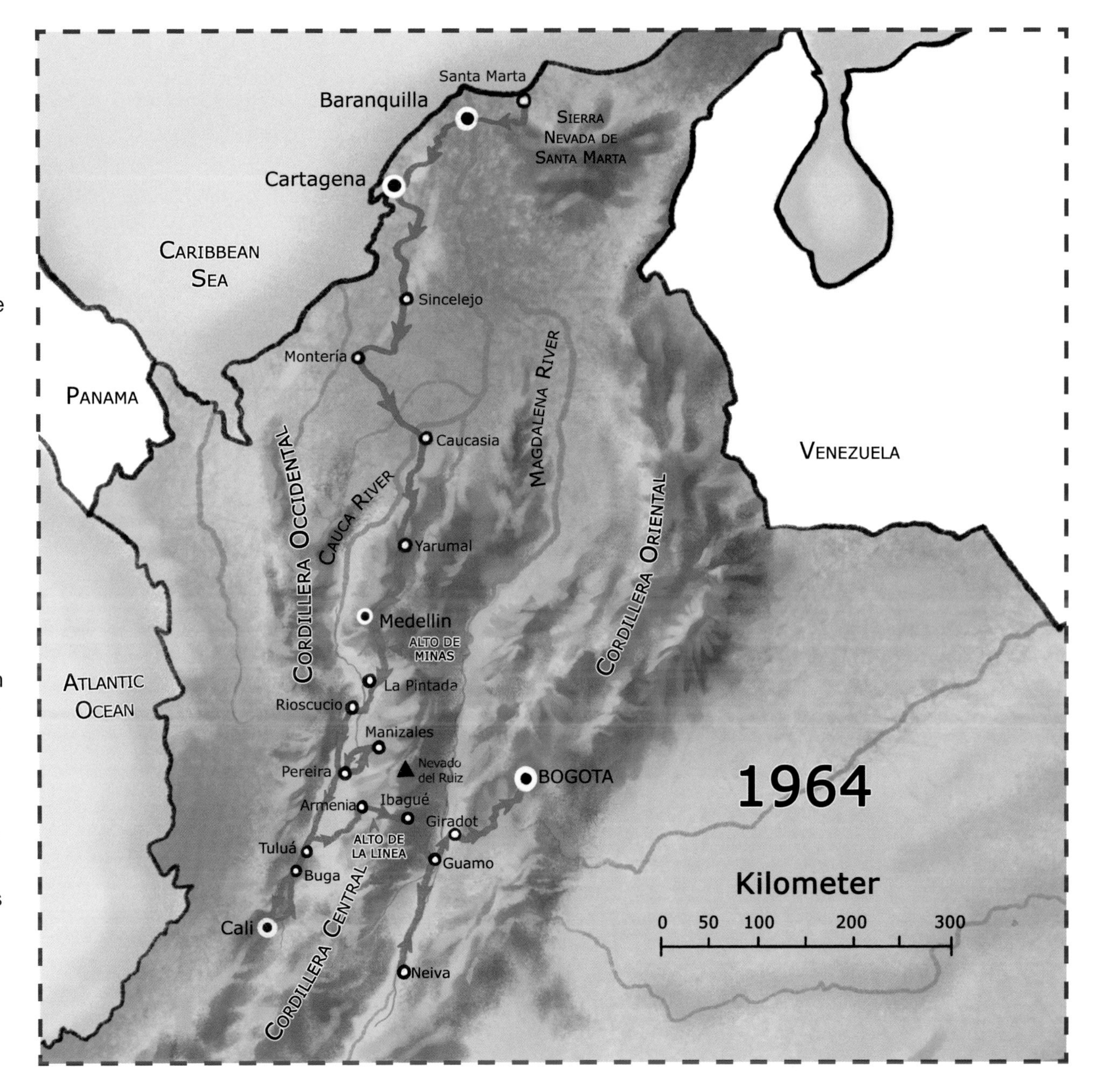


Route of the 1964 Vuelta a Colombia. *Copyright: Author. Created by Yoko Matsuoka*

## Roberto Buitrago Dueñas

### Born
13th January, 1937
in Guayatá,
Boyacá
Altitude 1,767m

### Nickname
Pajarito (little bird)

### Early days
Roberto Buitrago Dueñas was born in Guayatá, a small town on the mountainside of the Corderilla Oriental, close to the border with Cundinamarca. He was one of 12 children. When he was little, his parents moved to Bogota to escape La Violencia, the civil war that killed 200,000 people. He started riding, aged 8, on rented bikes and then he got a job as a messenger/delivery boy for a pharmacy and earned enough money to buy a racing bike.

### Vuelta a Colombia stages: 6

### Vuelta a Colombia podium
1962, but 2nd in 1960
and 3rd in 1961

### Career
His first official competition was the Doble a Suba. In 1956 he ran his first Vuelta a Colombia, for a Cundinamarcan team.
In 1957, aged 20, he won his first stage, over La Linea and was 2nd in the KOM. In 1960 he came second in the GC, but held the jersey for 12 stages in succession, a record that has never been bettered. Then in 1962, he finally won the Vuelta, and quit. Except that he got nostalgia and came back in 1965 – and wore the leader's jersey for one stage!

### Later days
After he retired, Roberto Buitrago got married and set up a cigar store in Bogota, which became famous for selling Soachan almojábanas, a popular kind of pastry.
Then for 20 years, he ran a business leasing heavy machinery, which he handed over to his only son, also called Roberto and a civil engineer. Nowadays, Buitrago owns a restaurant in Bogota, serving traditional dishes from his native Boyacá. Naturally it is called El Campeon.

### Grand Tour & Other wins
None

# 1964 The 1964 Vuelta was a monster.

Five of the top six finishers in the gruelling 1964 Vuelta seen here, urged on by their coaches. Cochise on the left, Gómez on his wheel, Suárez extreme right. *BPP., Medellin*

Not since Efraín Forero had anyone won by such a margin.

Nor did he leave crumbs on the table – his powerful physique enabled him to dominate both on the flat and the hills. The 15th stage of the race went over La Linea, one of the country's toughest climbs, and he won. His Antioquia 'A' team-mate Javier Suárez was 30 seconds behind him, and the next rider 4 minutes down. He was not just the GC winner, he was the King of the Mountains and – unusually – the intermediate sprints[2].

The Magdalena River near its mouth into the Caribbean Sea. There was no bridge in 1964 so the entire race took the ferry. Riders were timed on arrival at the eastern shore and re-leased at the same intervals on the other side. *Biblioteca Publica Piloto, Medellin*

Radio Caracol, "the voice of Antioquia" in action. *Biblioteca Publica Piloto, Medellin*

2 · Typically climbers are skinny with a big power to weight ratio, while sprinters are heavier, but with more muscle. Cochise excelled both as a climber and sprinter.

# Javier Amado Suárez

## Born
3rd November 1943
Don Matías, Antioquia
Altitude 2,600 metres

## Nickname
El Ñato (Snub nose!)

## Vuelta a Colombia podium
1965 (but 3rd 1962, 2nd 1966, 1967, 1968)

## Grand Tour & Other wins
Also won RCN Clásico 1965, 1966.

## Early days
Javier Suárez had a difficult start in life, like Cochise. Born in the small town of Don Matias, 50 kilometres from Medellin, he worked long hours in the fields. His mother – a single mother – moved to Medellin. Javier Suárez remembers his teacher lending him 300 pesos so he could buy copies of the El Colombiano newspaper which he sold on the street, and so earned some money for the family. He worked for a pharmacy, and earned his first bike from his employer. His big break came when he rode in a race that finished at half time during a soccer match in the Atanasio Giradot stadium.
His talent was noted by the directors of Sudamericana who offered him a job. It was the beginning of a long partnership.

## Career
While a lifelong friend of Cochise, he was also his greatest rival on the road, and famously beat him in the Vuelta in 1965. He was 3rd in the 1962 Vuelta, and then second in 1966, 1967 and 1968.

## Vuelta a Colombia stages: 10

## Later days
He could have ridden for longer, but contracted hepatitis in 1968 while competing in Mexico City. This debilitating condition forced him to retire from competition. He worked for La Sudamericana de Seguros in Medellin for many years. He refused to become a coach, saying that today's athletes are weak and do not have the dedication to the sport that he had. Not for him are late nights, drinking and smoking. A family man, he counts the happiest days of his life as April 4, 1965, when he won the Vuelta a Colombia, the day of his marriage to Laura and the day his daughter was born.

# 1965 Outside Colombia

Ramón Correa – from another team – shares his water with Javier Suárez who had run out (Clásico RCN 1966). The harsh conditions and physical privations created a great camaraderie between riders, regardless of which team they were in. *Biblioteca Publica Piloto, Medellin*

In 1965, for the first time in its history, the Vuelta ventured outside Colombia. It started in the Venezuelan city of San Cristobal. But in other respects it began like a rerun of 1964. Javier Suárez, Buitrago, Rubén Darío Gómez and Cochise were all in contention.

After winning the 5th stage, Cochise took the tricolour jersey on the 8th and held it. So far, so good. But his Antioquian teammate Javier Suárez was right up his tailpipes. At the end of Stage 13, Suárez was 6 minutes and 30 seconds behind the race leader. The 14th stage was a mountain stage, going over Santa Rosa. On the descent to Manizales, Suárez took off, accompanied by 3 others including Buitrago.

Cochise was in a following group. After a stunningly aggressive ride, Suárez won the stage and reduced Cochise's lead to 2 minutes 30. The next day he won again. Now Cochise's lead was down to 79 seconds.

The penultimate stage was a time trial and here Cochise fought back, taking his overall lead back up to 3 minutes and 34 seconds. The final day was a long 197 kilometres climb, up to Bogota and the stadium. Suárez took an early lead. For the last 100 kilometres, he cycled ahead. Cochise and a pack of eight riders were behind him. Suárez had no idea how far away they were. He crossed the finishing line and the crowd held its breath. As 3 minutes and 34 seconds came and went, the stadium erupted.

The Vuelta had a new hero, and his winning margin over Cochise was 1 minute 49 seconds. The commentators were quick to point out the flaws in their fallen hero, and contrast them with the virtues of the new one. "It was la dolce vita," cried El Tiempo, implying that Cochise had been seduced by 'easy living'. Though he denied it at the time, today Cochise admits there was some truth in it.

Vuelta a Colombia 1965, last day. Cochise on the climb from La Dorada, about to lose the Vuelta to Suárez. *Biblioteca Publica Piloto, Medellin*

Cochise had barely been in training for 2 months before the race, and had a busy social life. Suárez, on the other hand, didn't drink or smoke. He trained religiously and had built up to the Vuelta that year with three other races, all of which he had won.

Javier Suárez: rigid self discipline earned him the prize in the 1965 Vuelta. *BPP, Medellin*

Cochise (left) and Javier Suárez. Suárez was affectionately known as el Nato, "pugnose," a Colombian joke because his nose was anything but flat. *Biblioteca Publica Piloto, Medellin*

1966-1967

COCHISE, COCHISE, COCHISE

# The return of the chief

Cochise returned in 1966, determined to take back his crown. Fully fit and demonstrating his extraordinary strength both on the flat and in the mountains, he was unstoppable. By the time he arrived in his home town of Medellin, he had already won 6 of the 10 stages. Newspaper headlines just read: “La Vuelta, Martín Emilio’s Monopoly”.

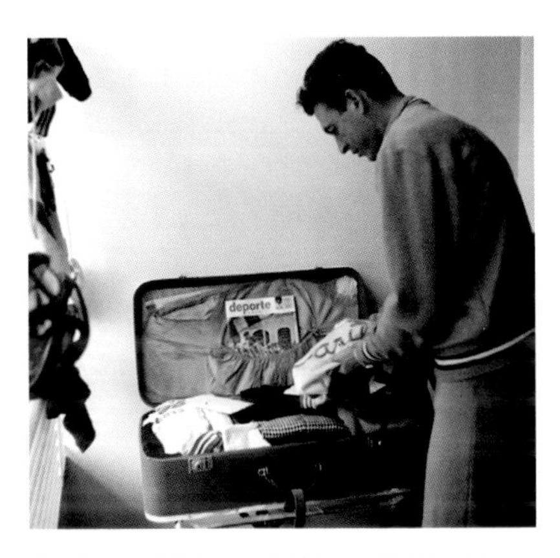

Cochise and his overnight bag *BPP, Medellin*

His teammate and rival Javier Suárez was the closest to him, but already 13 minutes down. Day after day, Cochise extended his lead, followed by Suárez. When he crossed the final stage on 30th May, 1966, he was 41 minutes ahead in the General Classification. He was also King of the Mountains and won the intermediate sprints contest. Suárez was second, and so naturally their team Antioquia ‘A’ won the team competition.

It was much the same in 1967. Cochise won four stages, including the Alto de Letras. His time over that great climb from Fresno to Manizales beat the previous record set by Ramón Hoyos in 1954 by an astonishing 26 minutes 53 seconds, admittedly on better roads.

Cochise also won the individual time trial by 1 minute and 35 seconds, and started the final stage with 14 minutes in hand, in front of Suárez.

Arrastia interviews the young Cochise
*Biblioteca Publica Piloto, Medellin*

Cochise hurtling down from the Alto de Letras in 1967 to set a new record.
*Biblioteca Publica Piloto, Medellin*

## Martín Emilio Cochise Rodríguez

### Born
14th April, 1942
Medellin
Altitude 1,500 metres

### Career
In 1961, he entered the RCN Clásico on its inaugural year and came second, behind Rubén Darío Gómez and with Hernán Medina in third place. That same year, he won a stage in the Vuelta and was also the leading novice. The next year, he lost the Vuelta by 8 seconds and then he won the race every year for the next 5 with the exception of 1985.
In 1963 he won the RCN Clásico as well!

### Nickname
Cochise, after the Apache Indian chief he admired in the film "Broken Arrow".

### Early days
Cochise's father died eleven days after the birth of his son and he was brought up by his mother. He had to work. He sold lemons and newspapers and delivered charcoal to householders. Like Roberto Buitrago, he got a job as bike messenger for a pharmacy. His first race was the Doble a Giradota. Riding a woman's bike, he made it there but cramp stopped him on the way back. He joined the Antioquian cycling team and trained with Javier Suárez.

### Vuelta a Colombia podium
1963, 1964, 1966, 1967
(but 2nd 1962, 1965, 1969)
and RCN Clásico (1963)

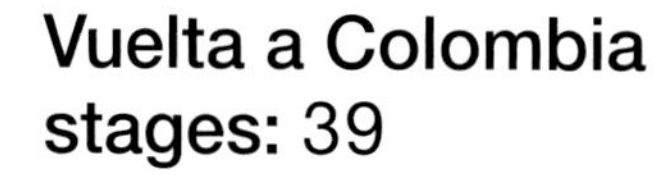

**Vuelta a Colombia stages:** 39

### Later days
He stopped winning in Colombia but far from retiring, he created a new career, competing abroad. He won a stage of the Giro d'Italia and the Trophy Barachi in 1973, and another stage in the Giro in 1975. Today he is the iconic symbol of the Colombian cycling success. For many years, he has coached and run the Colombian cycle team Coldeportes Zenú.

### Grand Tour & Other wins
Too many to list.
Holder of the Hour record (Mexico City 1970), Trofeo Baracchi 1973, 2 stages of the Giro d'Italia, GP Camaiore 1973…

# 1967-1968 The return of the chief

Vuelta a Colombia 1968: the peleton passing La Ermita church in Cali. *BPP, Medellin*

He almost lost it all! He had-stayed with friends the night before (instead of in a hotel under the eagle eye of the coach), and ate beans – not his usual diet – and was unwell all night. It is 200 long and mostly uphill kilometres from Ibague to Bogota. Unable to eat, he rode on an empty stomach.
At the top of the climb into Fusagasuga, he was so weak that he couldn't reach the food stored in his shirt. Two team–mates fed him by hand.

After 10 minutes the champion was restored and rode off, leaving his companions behind.

Suárez finished 9 minutes ahead of him, which was not enough. Cochise won the Vuelta by 5 minutes, with Suárez in second place.

The 1967 Vuelta was more evenly balanced than in previous years – 15 different riders shared stage wins in the 20 stages.

As it turned out, this was the last Vuelta that Cochise was going to win. The next year, 1968, he had a fall early in the race, and he was not on form. At least until the time trial. Here he awoke from slumber. His time was 19 seconds ahead of second place. His win did not improve his temper. He complained to the judges that his old rival, Ramón Hoyos, had obstructed him on a scooter.

Cochise ended the Vuelta in 7th place, 16 minutes behind the leader. Javier Suárez was in second place, yet again.

Ricardo Ovalle being fed by hand (Vuelta a Colombia 1965) *Biblioteca Publica Piloto, Medellin*

A rider emerging from a stream (1967 Vuelta a Colombia) *Biblioteca Publica Piloto, Medellin*

# Young in heart and mind

Cochise starting out… *Biblioteca Publica Piloto, Medellin*

1969: Cochise in his prime. *Biblioteca Publica Piloto, Medellin*

Above is a photo of Cochise, in his earliest years, and below, Cochise in his prime after dominating Colombian cycling for a decade. His rivals thought he was finished, but he was just changing gears. In 1970 he set the world record for the Hour (i.e. how far can you cycle in 60 minutes?) and went on to race successfully in Europe.

And today, *half a century later*, you can join Cochise most mornings down at the cycle track in Medellin. Be there at 6am and be ready to ride for an hour or two in the peleton of friends and admirers, circling at 40kph. *If you can.*

# 1969 The King is dead, long live the King

The 1969 Vuelta started better for Cochise. The third stage was over La Linea, the classic climb over the Central Cordillera. Cochise chased the race leader, Pablo Hernandez, over the pass. He was at that point in third place. But his descending was so skilful that he overtook the others and won the stage by a minute. “Well, at least we know he is better prepared than he was for the RCN,” remarked his old rival Ramón Hoyos cuttingly in his newspaper column.

Race leader Pablo Hernandez gets moral and physical support from his team up the Alto de Minas. *Biblioteca Publica Piloto, Medellin*

Pablo Hernandez and his sponsor, Pierce Watches! *Biblioteca Publica Piloto, Medellin*

1969 TV commercial celebrates Cochise's Vuelta victories and Wrangler jeans: “Wrangler is the champion of blue jeans, and the blue jeans of the champion!”

Hernandez himself had a bad moment going up the Alto de Minas and was saved by the support of his team–mate. (see photo).

Cochise fought bravely and won the time trial as well. But at the finish on the last day, he found himself 12 minutes behind Pablo Hernandez.

“I'm not going to do another one of these,” he announced, “…all the mediocre riders, and many good ones, stick to me like glue and when I've pulled them along for a hundred or so kilometres, then they piss off!”

He didn't quite mean it. In fact, he contested the Vuelta a Colombia on and off for the next decade, and he won a stage in 1980, aged 38!

Still, it was the end of the Sixties. It was also the end of Antioqueño domination. Cochise had appeared in 1961 and cut short the ambitions of Hernán Medina, Darío Gómez and Roberto Buitrago. Now, a new contender was about to appear from the backstreets of Bogota. He was young, he was angry and he was obsessed with winning. He was also incredibly fast. His name was Rafael Antonio Niño Munévar.

Pablo Hernandez is congratulated by Miss Colombia after winning the 1969 Vuelta. *Biblioteca Publica Piloto, Medellin*

# Pablo Enrique Hernández López

## Born
12th February, 1940
Suesca, Cundinarmarca
Altitude 2,584 metres

## Nickname
Pablito (little Paul)

## Vuelta a Colombia stages: 9

## Vuelta a Colombia podium
1969 (but 3rd 1963, 1964)

## Early days
Born high up on the Altiplano of Cundiboyacense, he moved to Pereira to live with his brother, although by then he had won several cycling competitions. One of his most famous races was the 1963 Vuelta, where he defeated Cochise over La Linea, but in the end came third after Cochise came back in the penultimate stage, a time trial, and won the final race to Bogota.

## Career
He was the national road racing champion in 1964, and runner up in the Vuelta a Guatemala, and competed in the Tokyo Olympics. He was one of the Pereira four, who brought glory to the city of Pereira through their conquest of the hegemony of Antioquia and Boyacá cycling. But his greatest moment came in 1969 when he won the Vuelta a Colombia.

## Grand Tour & Other wins
None

## Later days
He moved to Mexico where he lived for many years until his return to his home town of Pereira in 2014.

# 1970 The Vuelta of the Peace

Nationwide riots broke out after General Pinilla lost a general election. *Casa Editorial El Tiempo S.A.*

There was a general election in Colombia one week before the start of the Vuelta. General Rojas Pinilla, who had ruled the country at the time of the first Vuelta, was making a comeback as leader of a populist party, ANAPO. He was narrowly defeated – perhaps unfairly defeated.

His supporters were outraged. There were riots and the Army stepped in to keep the peace. The country was threatened with civil war, or a coup.

This clip celebrates the unifying role of cycling in Colombian culture and politics. Includes glimpses of Julio Arrastia and Cochise.

The Chairman of the Colombian Cycling Association – another General – announced that this Vuelta would go ahead, and it would be known as the Vuelta of the Peace.

It was also the international Vuelta. Teams from Switzerland, Belgium, Italy, Venezuela and even Russia were all competing. The podium after the first stage was entirely foreign. The winners of the first three stages were a Spaniard, a Belgian and an Italian.

Heat and dust rising in the 1970 Vuelta of the Peace. *Biblioteca Publica Piloto, Medellin*

...and spectators tried to help as well. *Biblioteca Publica Piloto, Medellin*

But the Colombians were just warming up. When they got to the mountains – and especially La Linea – the foreigners were gone, demoralised by the heat in the valleys and the endless climbs.

Also gone was Abelino Ortega, winner of the 5th stage, whose urine contained a “high concentration of amphetamines”.

They were replaced by 3 riders from Cundinamarca, the province surrounding Bogota. The leader was Francisco Triana, an experienced rider. Lying second was his teammate, the 20 year old novice Rafael Antonio Niño.

El Niño (“the Kid”) – as he was instantly named – had won the under–23 Vuelta a Colombia in January of that year.

El Niño did not enjoy the publicity that accompanied his precocious victory. *Biblioteca Publica Piloto, Medellin*

NEW KID IN TOWN

# The Vuelta of the Peace

Foreign riders struggled with the heat and the climbs. *Biblioteca Publica Piloto, Medellin*

The race reached Stage 9. It ran from Medellin, south over the Alto de Minas, down into La Pintada and up again over the Alto de Tigre. On this second climb, El Niño dropped Triana and descended in glorious isolation to the finish, almost six minutes ahead.

He was, aged 20, the race leader and he retained the jersey on the next, 10th stage.

The 11th stage was short but brutal, leading over the Alto de Letras from Manizales to Honda. Another of his teammates, Gustavo Rincon, won the stage and took the jersey. The next day was a time trial, 34 kilometres. It was baking hot and windy. El Niño took back 17 seconds.

As the riders set out on the final stage – La Dorada to Bogota – el Niño was 63 seconds behind.

The final climb of the day was from the picturesque little town of La Villeta up to the Alto de la Tribuna. The ascent was – and still is! – 1950 metres (6,435 feet) over 37 kilometres.

On this climb, el Niño broke away from the peleton and joined up with Miguel Samacá. He needed to finish 64 seconds ahead of Gustavo Rincon and the peleton, to win.

Together el Niño and Miguel Samacá ascended and entered the outskirts of Bogota. Samacá crossed the line in the El Campin stadium first, just ahead of el Niño.

The crowd held their breath. There was a huge burst of cheering as Gustavo Rincon in the tricolour jersey entered the stadium and crossed the line, 2 minutes and 6 seconds after El Niño. He had lost too much time. After 53 hours on the road, El Niño won the 1970 Vuelta by less than a minute. Not just General Classification. He was of course the novice champion, but also King of the Mountains and his team Cundinamarca A won the team prize.

Cochise meanwhile had had a bad fall on the descent into La Villeta and lost 16 minutes on the day, leaving him in 9th place overall.

El Niño was an instant celebrity, but he did not relish the public eye. El Tiempo's interviewer described him as "skinny, ungainly, dialogue is difficult, he seems to fear interviews more than his competitors!" He would talk, but not about the things they wanted to hear:

**Journalist:** What's the most important thing outside cycling?
**El Niño:** *To live alone, and to dedicate myself to cycling in peace.*
**Journalist:** And people?
**El Niño:** *People bore me. Generally I don't want to talk with anyone and I prefer that they don't talk with me.*

Rafael Antonio Niño was born into a poor family in the town of Cucaita. As a teenager, he had left his mother and Cucaita to look for work in the big city.

Alvaro Gómez prays before a race. He came second among Vuelta a Colombia Novices in 1970 and 10th overall, and won several stages during his career. *Biblioteca Publica Piloto, Medellin*

# Colombian nicknames

Apache chieftain Cochise (played by Jeff Chandler in the 1950 movie Broken Arrow) was so admired by young Martin Emilio Rodriguez that he became "Cochise". Seen here alongside James Stewart. *Photo Twentieth Century-Fox Film Corporation*

Like the British army, Colombians have a tradition of nicknames, and every Colombian cyclist soon acquired one, often followed by the name of their hometown. There was always a story behind a nickname.

Luis Herrera came from the hill town of Fusagasugá and worked in the municipal gardens. He was a skinny, pigeon chested man with the tenacity of the world's greatest climber. So *Luis* became *Lucho*, or the Fighter, and the newspapers delighted to call him "the little gardener of Fusagasugá."

Ernesto Gallego was "the flea" and José Antonio Agudelo was "Tomato" Agudelo. The chemistry student Hernán Medina was the Student Prince and Henry Cárdenas was Cebollito, the little onion.

Perhaps respect for the austere Ramón Hoyos prevented him from being nicknamed as a vegetable or an insect. He was known simply as "Don Ramón of Marinilla". Rafael Antonio Niño was naturally el Niño, the kid.

When he was ten years old, Martín Emilio Rodríguez saw the 1950 movie "Broken Arrow". His admiration for the heroic Apache chieftain Cochise, played by Jeff Chandler, was such that his friends nicknamed him Cochise and that is what he became to every Colombian. In 2011 he changed his name officially to Martín Emilio Cochise Rodríguez!

The practice may be on the wane – Nairo Quintana is known simply as Nairo.

Horacio Gil's photo shows an Antioquian cycling team in a cheerful mood. On the back he wrote: "Alberto Escobar and Gerardo Parra are the only ones whose names I can remember. The other are "The Pintica", "The Ñato", "Picalua", "the Pinta, "the Chicken," "the painter" and "Picodioro." They were riding in the Vuelta a Colombia and they were united in a single cause: Antioquia."
*Biblioteca Publica Piloto, Medellin*

# 1971/1972 Disappointment

The country was ready for another dose of stardom from el Niño when the Vuelta came around at the end of April the following year, especially since he had won the Clásico RCN just the month before.

But it was not to be. His team-mate, Alvaro Pachon, led the GC from start to finish, with el Niño lagging some 8 minutes behind.

The duelling continued in 1972. Cochise won the time trial, el Niño won the stage over the Alto de Minas but the overall winner was Miguel Samacá, the climber who had helped el Niño to his first victory on the last day.

What did it all mean? Was his first precocious victory just a flash in the pan?

Miguel Samacá was a huge talent whose career was overshadowed by the "monsters": Cochise and el Niño. *BPP, Medellin*

# What it takes to be a Champion

*Over time, most successful athletes turn their early history into comfortable mythology. El Niño gave this interview to El Tiempo just a few days after winning his first Vuelta a Colombia. His words here reflect the authentic anger of youth without the sepia tint of recollection. It is humbling to read the obsessive dedication which created one of Colombia's greatest champions.*

El Niño came from the backstreets of Bogota to dominate Colombian cycling for a decade. *Biblioteca Publica Piloto, Medellin*

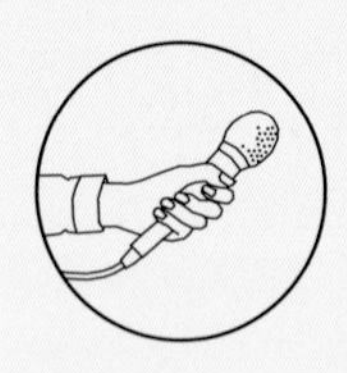

The day I bought my first bike, I walked home with it and put it in the patio. I already had prepared petrol, hessian and a few rags and, because I had flirted with it for so long, I knew exactly what the flaws were. I cleaned it completely, even the pedals, and then, I finally got on it.

I didn't go to work that day, I went round the streets. I rode as fast as I could. I got off it around 11 o'clock that night, exhausted, but didn't go to sleep. First I washed and cleaned it again, and greased it. It made me sad to leave it in the patio in case it rained but it didn't fit in my room. It's just that ever since I have lived alone in a room, I have left my bicycle inside. I don't know if it's the downpour or the affection. But I don't like it sleeping outside.

**The big sacrifice**

I don't know why I like shirts so much. It must be because when I was a kid I only had one I liked. So since I began earning, the thing I would buy the most were shirts. But in those days, when I had managed to get my bike, I had to save much more so I could afford the spare parts. In a store in Ricaurte, there were two beautiful shirts that I would look at every day through the shop window. I didn't buy them in order to put calipers on my bike. It was a huge sacrifice for me. But I preferred my bike.

I would ride from home to Ricaurte. It took me a half hour. I would come home for lunch just because I had the riding frenzy. Just riding to work and back was a two hour ride. But at night, I would ride until eleven or twelve and that caused me problems which made me angry because I was not made to live in grief.

**I could not see the money.**

I left my job at the repair shop because I now I had my bike.... I was out of a job for fifteen days. I was really worried because I had no money. Then I got a job as a messenger boy – the one I thought I had always wanted – at the Electra chemist. I was given the area around 57th street... uphill always.
These neighbourhoods are high up and the streets are steep. At the beginning it was a huge effort to deliver the goods because the streets were very steep. I had to make huge efforts and it wore me out. Ha. But a month later I got into it and could cope well.

next left page

# 1973 A close run thing

Cochise was missing from the starting line in 1973. He had moved onto the next stage of his glorious career and was in Europe, competing in Italy (his first European victory, in fact, the Grand Prix City of Camaiore).

Rafael Niño had joined the Cundinamarca Nectar team, along with Triana. Three of his strongest opponents (Morales, Samacá and Pachon) had joined a rival team, Cundinamarca-Singer. The pack set off to ride to Cali. When they got to the small town of Puerto Tejada, their route was blocked by an angry protest against the government and the organisers cut it short.

The next day was a time trial, followed by a road race around Cali. El Niño won the time trial, and took the leaders jersey. The next day, he lost it on a long, flat stage.

Stage 6 was the Stage of Death, from Riosucio north to Medellin. El Niño won it by 2 minutes and 30 seconds from his old rival, Miguel Samacá, and took the jersey.

On the 12th stage, still in the tricolour jersey, he descended La Linea in a lead group of six cyclists, including his rivals Alvaro Pachon and Miguel Samacá. Pachon, who had won the stage the day before, was in the lead and driving hard. El Niño slipped on gravel and went down. Miguel Samacá was right behind him and fell as well but got up and carried on.

Niño staggered up. He had damaged his right cheek and blood was flowing from it, and banged his left knee and thigh. He got back on his bike and tried to catch up the descending group. But the Singer team (Morales, Samacá and Pachon) were not about to let him in. They all finished ahead of him.

Abelardo Rios with wife and daughter (Vuelta a Colombia 1973). *Biblioteca Publica Piloto, Medellin*

Suárez injured, being supported by his trainer. Date unknown. *Biblioteca Publica Piloto, Medellin*

# What it takes to be a Champion

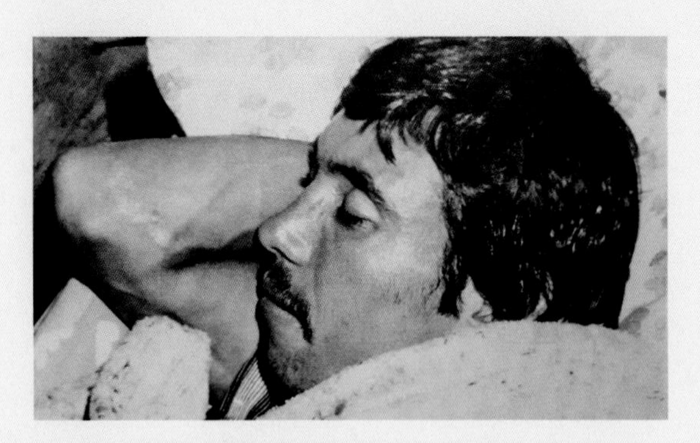

El Niño: six times winner of the Vuelta a Colombia in repose
*Biblioteca Publica Piloto, Medellin*

from previous left page

At the chemist's they liked me because I was the only one who stuck it out with the work in that patch. Before me, the messengers didn't last longer than a week... I lasted there. I lasted around a year or more.

In the end, I would climb really fast. I would sweat all day. In that line of work, sweat is a nuisance at first. It is unpleasant to be soaked from morning to evening. But in the end one gets used to it, even the smell on your clothes...that has made me very clean. Often I would bathe twice and change my clothes.

It was embarrassing to arrive at those luxurious homes with a sweaty face. I felt very small when the ladies walked out to receive their package. They were nice to me. Within six months they knew me by name in some places and called me Rafa and gave me good tips. But I would spend them or give them to the poor children. I was never able to save any money. That is why I think I am neither stingy nor selfish.

**I dreamt of a house of my own.**
At work I was happy though not all the time because I suffered when I saw beautiful women who lived around there. I liked them a lot but was just a messenger boy and they were rich girls...

To make things worse, it got complicated at home and, gradually I became unhappier. It's just that what happened around me has always affected me. If I have arguments or differences with people, I get angry: and then become really sad. It lasts throughout the day.

**Alas! A place of my own.**
I am a rebel and at home, they pestered me, for example, because I was late. I worked until 10 at night, rain or shine, so, sometimes I just went to bed without supper. And often, I didn't sleep because I was hungry. I would get up at midnight and drink water but had nothing to eat.

My life became hard, so I asked my sister Marina to put me up. She lives in La Estrada. She said yes and I left immediately. I was overjoyed to see that I'd have a room to myself. It was the first time in my life that I had a room of my own, just like I'd always wanted.
I think that I was able to regain my calm for a few months. The only problem was at night, because I was afraid to ride home and have my bike stolen...

During those days, I bought my first bed, with no bedside table because I didn't have enough. I felt very happy to have a bed of my own. It was made of metal and I acquired it at a store in town.

## The Lady Lastenia

For many years, when the race arrived in Manizales, an old lady would appear with presents of little bags of fruit. She gave her name as Lastenia López. No one knew where she came from or why she did it. She became a kindly fixture. Here she is being affectionately thanked by Luis A. Muñoz.

# 1973 A close run thing

As they set out the next morning on the gruelling final climb into Bogota, el Niño's lead was down to 2 minutes and 10 seconds over Samacá, who had won the year before.

"We're going full on for Bogota," the Singer team announced to the press, "to win or to die." And their coach Efraín Forero – the revered Father of the Vuelta, agreed: "Win or die. Yes, I would prefer that the lads all die, rather than give up their attack on the Vuelta. We will go on the attack, it has to be like that."

So the whole nation was, metaphorically, on the edge of their seats at 9.30am the next morning. It was a morning of constant attacks, as the Singer team tried to drop el Niño. But he stuck doggedly with them, up the long climb. He and Samacá crossed the finish line in a group. It was all he needed. He was, aged 23, and for the second time, the GC champion of the Vuelta a Colombia.

The next year, lured by the glory of racing abroad, Niño turned professional and went to Europe. He joined an Italian team and rode in the Giro alongside Giovanni Battaglin, but it was not a success. He did not have Cochise's easy going temperament and he was not happy away from Colombia.

Accident on road. *Biblioteca Publica Piloto, Medellin*

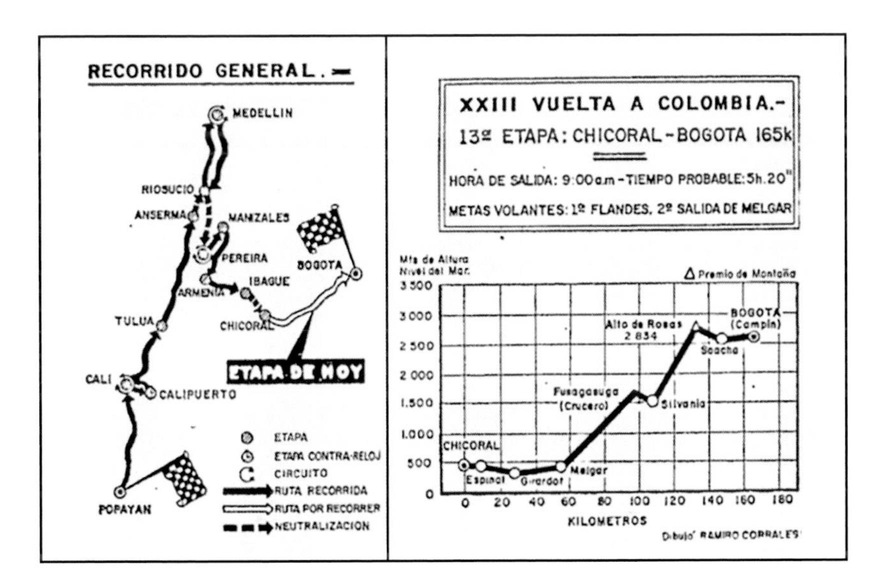


1973 Vuelta. Course Route and altimetría for the final stage. *Casa Editorial El Tiempo S.A.*

This little group may be watching Samacá and the Singer team duelling it out with el Niño *Biblioteca Publica Piloto, Medellin*

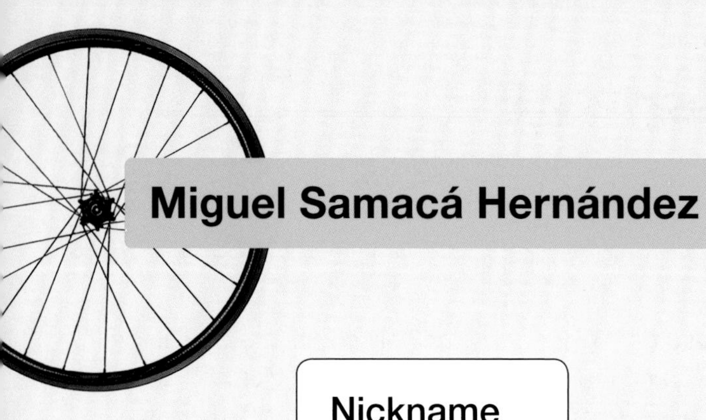

# Miguel Samacá Hernández

**Born**
18th May 1946
Tuta, Boyacá
Altitude 2,600 metres

**Nickname**
Don Coraje
"Don Courage"

**Vuelta a Colombia stages:** 9

**Vuelta a Colombia podium**
2 (1972, 1974). He was on the podium 5 times (2 x 1st, 2 x 2nd, 1 x 3rd).

**Early days**
Good on the flat, and also on the mountains, he came 3rd in the Novice section of the Vuelta in 1966.

**Career**
He competed in the Vuelta a Colombia 11 years in succession, with great success winning it outright in 1972 and 1974, although this second victory was due to the disqualification of the "first past the post" Alvaro Pachon who tested positive for amphetamines.

**Later days**
For the last 30 years, Miguel Samacá has run a bicycle shop in Bogota.

**Grand Tour & Other wins**
None. He competed in 3 Olympics (1968, 1972, 1976).

# 1974 Doping and disappointment

The 1974 Vuelta started up on the Caribbean coast, and rode down past the ancient seaport of Cartagena, reaching Medellin on the 5th day. Alvaro Pachon, still riding for Singer, dominated the race from the moment it reached the mountains after Medellin, closely followed by his old team-mate Miguel Samacá.

Pachon won the penultimate stage, the big climb over the Alto de La Línea from Armenia to Ibague, but Samacá triumphed the next day and came first into the stadium at Bogota, but not far enough ahead to win the GC.

The next day the Cycling Federation announced that Pachon had tested positive for amphetamines and he was disqualified.

He and his coach, the legendary Efraín Forero, cheekily told the media that Samacá had given Pachon some of his rations on the descent from Letras, and maybe this was how the amphetamines had got into his bloodstream!

The media loved it, but the Federation were not impressed, especially as Pachon had failed a drugs test back in 1971 when he won the Clásico RCN. (On that occasion, the precocious Rafael Niño was declared winner instead!). Pachon was disqualified and Samacá declared the winner of the 1974 Vuelta.

1974: Alvaro Pachon holds high the Vuelta Cup. Does he look worried? The next day he was disqualified for doping.
*Casa Editorial El Tiempo S.A.*

# Inside the cobbler's shop

Biblioteca Publica Piloto, Medellin

It wasn't just the bikes and the riders who suffered from the conditions on the roads, but their footwear as well. Here we see a queue of cyclists outside the shop of cobbler Jacob Jaramillo...

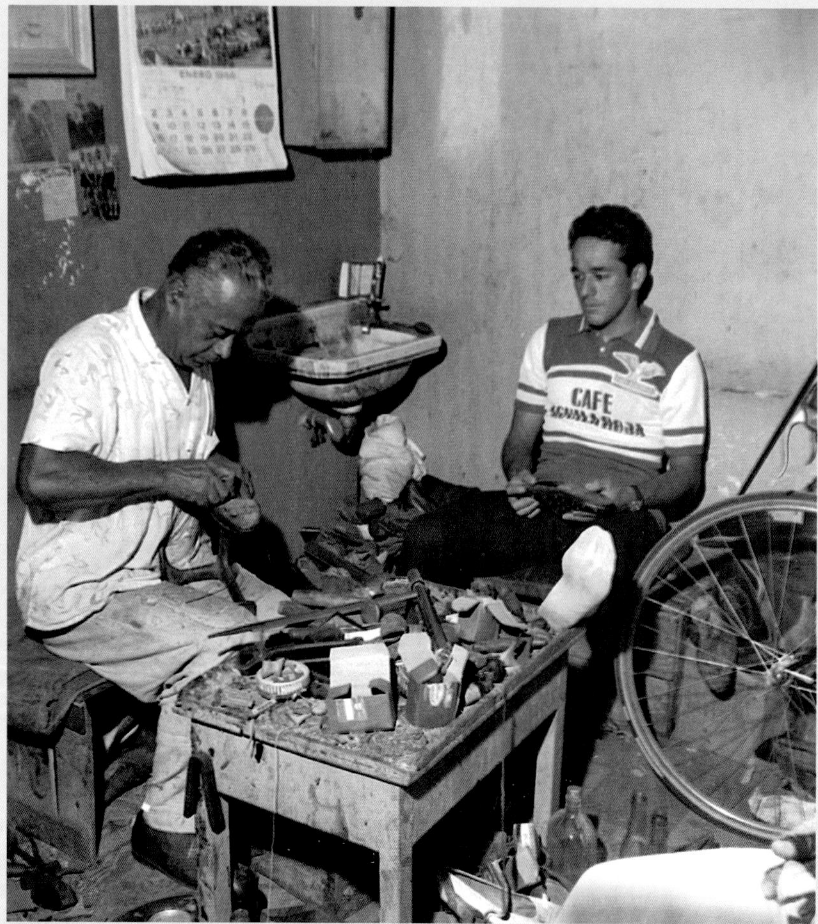

Biblioteca Publica Piloto, Medellin

And inside, Jaramillo himself and the rider Jaime Ospina having his cycling shoes repaired!

# 1975 Dawn of the Industrial Age

Crop spraying plane takes a closer look at the Vuelta. z

Rafael Niño returned from Europe in 1974 without prizes or glory. But he was fired up with new ideas about how a cycling team should be organised and trained along professional lines. With characteristic single-mindedness, he set about it.

First, the money. He found two sponsors with deep pockets – one of them a bank – and then began assembling a complete team along European lines.

After the money, the riders. The team he picked was not the most outstanding of Colombian riders, but they bunch need to be. Their job to be there for the boss. To feed him, shelter him and give him a new bike the moment he had a puncture.

Then there was the riders' diet. The team was not going to eat hotel food like the other teams. It had its own cook and dietician, one Diogenes Beltran. And its own doctor, William Jiménez, an ex-cyclist, who had identified and treated Rafael Niño for anaemia.

# Rafael Antonio Niño Munévar

## Nickname
El Niño de Cucaita

## Grand Tour & Other wins
Also won the RCN Clásico 1971, 1975, 1977, 1978.

## Early days
El Niño's family moved to Bogota from the country, like so many, during the Violencia when he was 11. His sister got him a job in a repair shop. He saved up to buy his first bike which he adored. He listened to cycling on the radio and his idol was Alvaro Pachon. Then he worked as a delivery boy for a pharmacy. Unhappy at home, he would ride his bike into the small hours. Eventually he moved out to live with his sister. He joined a club and started riding in local competitions. He burst into the national scene when he won the Juventidad – the youth cycling Vuelta – and then went on to win the Vuelta in the same year, aged 20.

## Born
11th December, 1949
Cucaita, Boyacá
Altitude 2,650 metres

## Vuelta a Colombia podium
1970, 1973, 1975, 1977, 1978, 1980 (but 3rd 1971).

## Vuelta a Colombia stages: 11

## Career
El Niño dominated the Colombian road racing through the 1970s. After his early victories in Colombia in 1970-73, he was invited to compete in Europe in 1974. He didn't enjoy it. He finished 17th in the Tour de Suisse and 41st in the Giro d'Italia, but he came home with strong ideas about how a team should be managed. He created a highly successful organisation, and won the Vuelta a Colombia four more times, and RCN Clásico three times.

## Later days
After he retired, he became the coach of the Café de Colombia professional team which competed in Europe throughout the 1980s with great success. In later years, through the influence of his friend Zorro Hernandez, he became a Christian and married again. He continues to manage and train a domestic team.

# 1975 Dawn of the Industrial Age

Supplementing the doctor and dietician was a peculiarly Colombian addition, an "inyectologo," or a man who gives injections. In this case, injections of vitamins and mineral supplements necessary to keep the team in peak performance. Rounding out the medical team was "Pepe." Pepe – Ricardo Soto was his real name – was said to be the best masseuse in Colombian cycling, a reputation he gained by looking after Cochise in the 60s.

Fabio Duarte and son in their bike shop in Bogota in front of a frame building harness. *Photo: author*

Rafael Niño was a perfectionist along every dimension. He engaged a top mechanic, José Duarte to look after the bikes. Such was his trust in Duarte that before long, he was asking him to refactor the frames of his bikes. Duarte did, and went on to create a frame building business. By 1980 half the peleton was riding on his frames – and el Niño won 5 of his 6 victories using them. During the race, the team was supported by two motorcycles. The first carried a mechanic, spares and supplies. The second enabled Marcel Plaz, head coach and tactician, to see what was going on, and to direct the tactics of the team.

It worked. Rafael Niño won the Vuelta in 1975, 1977, 1978 and 1980. And he won the other most prestigious Colombian race, the Clásico RCN, four times over the same period. It could have been more, but a knee injury kept him out of both competitions in 1976.

Elkin Darío Rendon, who later became the assistant coach of the Postobon team, waits for a wheel change. He was a good friend of Alfonso Flórez and was himself murdered in Medellin in 1999. *BPP, Medellin*

# The clásico RCN

Pascal Simon, Flórez and Greg Lemond raced together in Colombia in the 1980s. *Photo El Colombiano*

The success of the Vuelta a Colombia bred rivals. In 1961, RCN, one of the major radio networks in Colombia, decided to sponsor their own race. For the first six years, the event was run over two days but from 1966 it was extended to ten stages. It ran over many of the same climbs as the Vuelta including Letras, La Linea, Alto de Tigre etc.

Due to its sponsorship, it soon became a major event, rivalling and perhaps surpassing its big sister the Vuelta in prestige.

Its finest years were the 1980s, when Lucho Herrera and Fabio Parra were riding. Because it was run early in the year (March to May), it was perfect for European riders who wanted to train at altitude early in their season.

During the 1980s, many of the great Europeans competed and won stages in the RCN, including Bernard Hinault, Pascal Simon, Sean Kelly and Laurent Fignon.

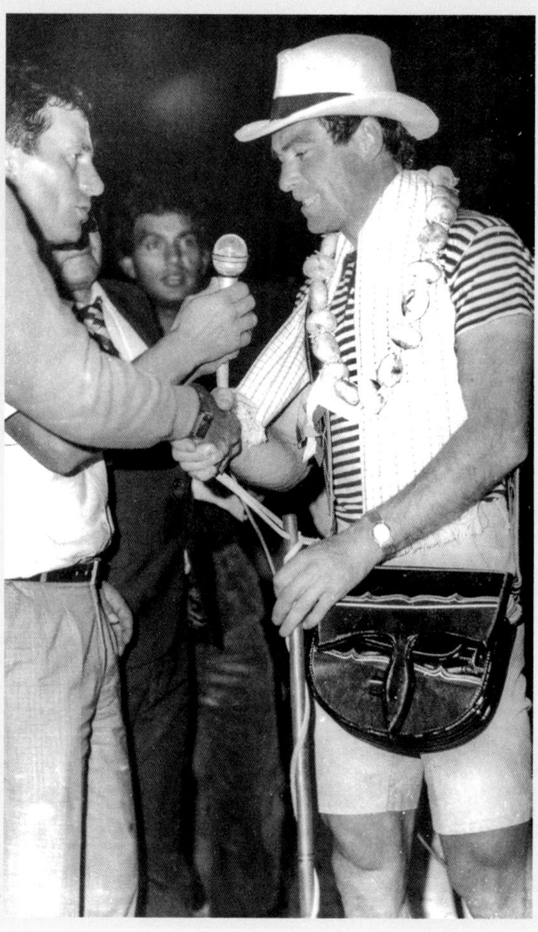

Bernard Hinault as a cowboy at a celebration, probably in Antioquia
*Biblioteca Publica Piloto, Medellin*

# 1976

NEW KID IN TOWN

# Patro's year

Patrocinio Jiménez after a tough day on the road. *Photo Hervasquez*

Niño's injury in 1976 gave space to Patrocinio (aka "Patro") Jiménez, who was "subcampeón" to Niño in 1975.

The Vuelta did not start well for Jiménez – he lost 8 minutes to his team-mate, Plinio Casas. So he was ordered to ride for Casas. The next day, the race went over La Linea. The team director told him to attack, to wear out the competition. He obeyed with enthusiasm, arriving in Pereira not only ahead of the competition, but seven and a half minutes ahead of team-mate Casas.

Plinio Casas was less than a minute ahead of Jiménez as they came to the final stage from Riosucio to Medellin over the Alto de Minas. Here the team director gave his sparring riders carte blanche to slog it out: "May the best man win."

Patrocinio Jiménez won the stage by 7 minutes – and with it, the Vuelta.

The following year, el Niño was back and Patro Jiménez was back to second, yet again!

El Niño and the team machine he had created dominated Colombian road racing from 1974 to 1980. After the disappointments of 1974, he never went back to race in Europe.

Others did. The great Cochise, outgoing and gregarious, aspired to international success and built the friendships and contacts to make them possible. He set the Hour record in Mexico City in 1970, and won the 4,000 metre individual track pursuit at the World Championships in 1971.

Patrocinio Jiménez (front) Abelardo Rios (middle) and Antonio Flórez (back) on rough ground and uphill. *Biblioteca Publica Piloto, Medellin*

Cochise also competed as a domestique in the Tour de France in 1975, finishing 27th, and he continued to ride in the Vuelta whenever fitness allowed. He won his final stage in 1980, aged 38.

*Mexico City, 7th October 1970: The big board tells the story.* Cochise has just set a new world record of 47.566 kilometres in one hour. *Biblioteca Publica Piloto, Medellin*

# José Patrocinio Jiménez Bautista

## Born
17th January, 1953
Ramiriqui, Boyacá
Altitude 2,325 metres

## Nickname
Patro.

## Vuelta a Colombia stages:
3 stage wins but King of the Mountains 1976, 1979, 1980, 1981.

## Grand Tour & Other wins
3rd in Tour de l'Avenir 1981, won Coors Classic 1982, 4xTour de France including 2nd place KOM 1983, 3xVuelta a España.

## Vuelta a Colombia podium
Won in 1976 (and KOM) 2nd 1975, 3rd 1979, 1980, 1983

## Early days
Aged 13, driven out by violence and poverty, he migrated to Bogota with his twin brother, and joined his father and 2 brothers. He found work in construction, where the workers listened to the Vuelta a Colombia all day on the radio. His hero was Cochise, of course. His brother got him a bike, and they used to get up at 3am to go training on the streets of Bogota, before work started at 7am. He won some local races. He slept with his bike next to him and swore that come rain or lightning, he would train for 5 hours every day.

## Career
"Patro" won the Vuelta a Juventidad (the Colombian race for under 22s) in 1974, but his promising career was overshadowed by the monster talent of el Niño and his team. In 1975, he was subcampeon to Niño. In 1976 Niño was injured and Patro won everything: the Vuelta, the Clásico RCN, the Vuelta a Tachira. In 1977, Niño was back and Patro was back to subcampeon! He finished the Vuelta a Colombia 8 times.

He had many road racing successes around Latin America, and went on to win stages in the Tour de l'Avenir and other European races. In 1983 he joined the Great Adventure with Alfonso Flórez. Flórez abandoned before the mountains, but Jiménez persisted, fighting a famous battle with Robert Millar in the Pyrenees, and he wore the King of the Mountains jersey for 5 days.

He rode in support of Herrera and Parra in 4 Tour de France and 3 Vuelta a España. He twice won the prize of "amabilite" – likeable fellow – in the Tour de France! In 19 years of racing, he never broke a bone or had a serious accident – which he ascribes to luck and learning how to fall.

## Later days
Patrocinio Jiménez is still engaged in the Colombian domestic cycling scene, transporting journalists and photographers around the Vuelta, the RCN Clásico and other races.

NEW KID IN TOWN

# 1979 The steel horse

Is she helping? Probably. *Biblioteca Publica Piloto, Medellin*

The 1979 Vuelta was won by a man whose tragic end has overshadowed his lifetime achievements.

Efraín Forero, Ramón Hoyos, Cochise and el Niño were superlative young riders who made onto the podium aged 19 or 20. Alfonso Flórez Ortiz by contrast was a slow developer. Like the Colombian climbs, you might say, his career was long but finished very high up. He came from Bucaramanga in the department of Santander. He wanted to be an athlete but gave it up after a disappointing race. Then he tried soccer. He didn't seem committed to anything except his reputation as a ladies' man. And then he won a touring bike in a raffle, and became a passionate cyclist.

Gritty and courageous, he seemed at his best in extreme weather conditions. He started with two stages of the 1974 Vuelta, aged 21. Like Cochise, he could climb, but he was also powerful on the flat. The first win was on a long stage downhill to the Caribbean coast.

Then a few days later, he won the stage of death over Las Minas from Medellin to Riosucio.

In 1976 he won two more stages, both sprint stages ridden in sweltering heat in the south of the country.

In 1977 he finished 3rd in the Vuelta, and in 1978 2nd, without winning a stage on either occasion. El Niño was of course the winner both years.

But 1979 was different. The 10th stage of the 1979 Vuelta was an individual time trial, held down in Cali. Driving into the pouring rain, Flórez won the race, defeating el Niño, his team mate Gonzalo Marin and the array of Colombian talent facing him. The rain was so intense that the second session, a 115 kilometre ride to Palmira, was cancelled.

Alfonso Flórez. *Biblioteca Publica Piloto, Medellin*

AROUND COLOMBIA

# Santander, mountain playground

Barichara, a colonial jewel of a town above San Gil
*Photo colombiacycling.com*

Santander is a mountainous department sitting to the north of Boyacá. On its western side, like Boyacá, it drops down off the Cordillera Oriental and meets Antioquia at the Magdalene River. Much of it is a jumble of steep peaks and vertiginous descents into river canyons.

It is to Colombia what Queenstown is to New Zealand: the place you go to do crazy extreme things. In Pescaderito, you can go white-water rafting, kayaking, bungie jumping, paragliding and potholing. In the little town of Salto de Mico, you have an opportunity to rapel down a waterfall 150 foot high. Or you can camp and hike round the Parque Nacional de Chicamocha and take the cable car across the Chicamocha Canyon (think Grand Canyon). The ride is over 6 kilometres long, one of the longest cable cars in the world.

As always in Colombia, the roads are mostly good and you can explore by bike or take your mountain bike.Santander also has one of Colombia's prettiest destinations, the tiny colonial town of Barichara, set on top of a mountain up above San Gil. The immaculately kept steep cobbled streets are charming and the people are friendly.

The capital of Santander is Bucaramanga, a modern city of 600,000 people which calls itself "the city of parks" because of the amount of green space. Bucaramanga was the boyhood home of Antonio Flórez.

Sunset over the mountains *Illustration based on Photo Cyclota.com*

### *Cycling notes*

*Riders looking for big climbs can pedal out of Bucaramanga, heading east towards the Venezuelan border. Before too long, the road heads up towards the Alto de Picacho. This long climb starts at 1,000 metres and finishes at 3,124 metres, 46 kilometres later!*

# 1979 The steel horse

Two days later, on the final stage, Niño attacked and dropped the race leader, Gonzalo Marin, who was Flórez's team-mate.

Against the orders of the team coach (because his job was to hang around and support Marin), Flórez went after Niño. Their 2 man breakaway sped up the mountains to Bogota. They finished over 4 minutes ahead of Marin, giving Flórez overall victory in the 1979 Vuelta by 45 seconds.

It was a great and unexpected achievement, but not one that made him popular with the betting public. Which was a big problem, because by 1979, the Colombian betting public was enormously rich, violent and well provided with *sicarios* (that is to say, professional assassins). And the deposed favourite, Gonzalo Marin, was close to the Escobar family.

Matt Rendell, in his book *Kings of the Mountains* writes that there were rumours of death threats against Flórez, stories of executioners contracted and then released and that Pablo Escobar himself [3] intervened to cool the tempers of those who had suffered enormous losses.

Fortunately for the history and glory of Colombian cycling, Flórez survived this particular escapade.

The peleton passing under a famous landmark, “la nariz”, a huge overhanging rock shaped like a nose (date unknown). *Biblioteca Publica Piloto, Medellin*

Antonio Londono takes the chequered flag in a tight finish (c. 1980, location unknown) *BPP, Medellin*

3. Escobar's involvement seems plausible. Gonzalo Marin for some years rode for Roberto Escobar and was related to the Escobars by marriage. He was later found on 25th April 1990, strangled in a barber's shop, presumed murdered by Los Pepes, the vigilante group who were assassinating members or associates of the Medellin cartel.

# Radio, more radio and TV

Jairo Garzón *Photo Jairo Garzón*

*During the 2018 Vuelta, we met up with Jairo Garzón, RCN Medellin narrator and sports reporter. Jairo had just finished a long day's commentary on the Vuelta but his enthusiasm for the sport and his job was undimmed.*

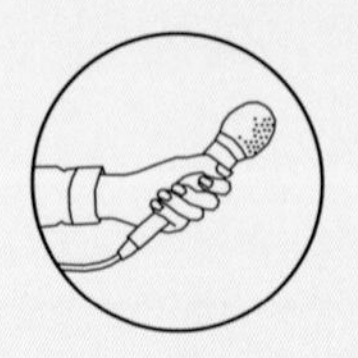

***What part did radio broadcasting play in the development of Colombian cycling?***

The Vuelta a Colombia could not have gripped the entire nation as it did in the 1950s without the radio. Radio was uniquely important – and remains important – in a mountainous country with a substantial farming community. You can *listen* to the race while rounding up a herd of cattle, but you cannot *watch* it.

In fact, TV coverage via helicopter did not arrive until 1985.

***This Vuelta radio tradition - how did it start?***

The pioneers were Carlos Arturo Rueda, a Costa Rican, and Julio Arrastia Brinca, an Argentine who was called the Bible of cycling.

Not forgetting Darío Alvarez, Alberto Piedrahita Pacheco and Rubén Darío Arcila.

A short account of Colombian radio and TV coverage. At the beginning, you can briefly hear Carlos Arturo Rueda in full voice as cycling commentator

Julio Arrastia, "the Bible of cycling." *BPP,Medellin*

These folks were the great innovators of sports radio broadcasting in Colombia.

And then in the next generation, we have Hector Urrego. Hector and his family have been a driving force in Colombian cycling journalism since the 1970s, along with his colleague Alberto Martinez who was unfortunately killed while broadcasting in 2006.

***You seem to talk at high speed for hours. How do you manage it?***

It's a skill! I think it started with Carlos Arturo Rueda. Carlos arrived in Colombia from Costa Rica. He was a soccer commentator and he brought the excitement and energy of soccer reportage to cycle racing, a very different kind of event.

There are lots of stories from the 1950s. To start with the reporting was done by telephone, so the commentator would go ahead in a car and invent the race! Or someone told them about the race while they waited at the finish. And they would replay what had happened in the race as if it was happening in front of them.

Carlos Arturo Rueda amusingly describes how he used his "magic brain" to create "live coverage" from a telephone at the finish.

***It sounds – well – stressful and probably inaccurate?***

It was. Both. So Carlos Arturo Rueda and crew pioneered the development of the transmovil, a specially designed mobile truck with an observation platform and built-in radio transmitters.

The big radio stations would have two, one going in front of the riders, and the other at the back. Nowadays we have a motorbike in the middle as well, because the race director won't let the transmovils get too close. The motorcycle is among the riders and tells us the inside story. That's important. The helicopter is for the TV.

The 20 strong Radio Caracol commentary team c. 1974
*Biblioteca Publica Piloto, Medellin*

***So the reporting has become strictly factual?***

We might call it "magical realism". The Vuelta in Colombia in the early days had no paved roads, it was practically cross-country and the riders in some sectors of the race went with the bike on their shoulders. So the richness of the radio, the richness of the language meant that cycling began to have a metaphorical meaning. It told a story to the audience who were glued to their radio.

That is the magic. The radio still retains a lot of magic because it's up to us to draw the listener into what is happening in the race.

We start almost from when the cyclists get up until they go to bed. Even during the afternoon and at night, there are cycling programs where people talk about what happened in the race, where the coaches talk about the medical part, the recovery and all the many aspects of cycling.

We might start with the support team and the mechanics, who get up 4 hours before the cyclists. If the cyclists are up at 6am, these guys are up at 2am, organizing bicycles, food, water, spare bikes and wheels. Loading the support vehicles. When each stage ends, the riders can relax, but for the mechanics, coaches and drivers, the work of preparing for the next day begins.

The team doctor also will be constantly checking his riders. Cycling is the only sport that when a stage is finished and on the day of rest, cyclists are still practicing 150 kilometres . It's amazing. When other sports such as the marathon finish, the runner waits a month or two before he gets back on the track!

***Do you know the Eurosport cycling commentators? How would you describe the difference between Colombian style and the European one?***

The style of the Colombian commentary is very tropical. It owes its flavour and warmth to the Caribbean.

next left page

# Radio, more radio and TV

Hector Urrego, the best known radio commentator in Colombia today, started his career in the 1960s. Here he interviews Dr. Vinicius Echeverry, a doctor whose Mediofondo cycling club nurtured a whole generation of Antioquian stars. *BPP, Medellin*

from previous left page

From the Caribbean, for example, we inherit the "g-g-g-g-g-goooal" in football. Although a bike race is longer than a soccer match, we create excitement from the beginning. From the moment the race starts, we talk with the tone up ... the listener is more engaged. The European commentators are much colder. So it seems to me!

***Nowadays you have TV coverage. Why is radio still important?***

TV is important, especially in the cities. Because a picture is worth a thousand words. But the radio still has that magic ... it is difficult to carry a television in the car or work while the radio is within reach, especially in Colombia which is very rural. Many people live in the countryside and most cyclists come from the countryside. Their families and neighbours want to listen.

A transmovil in Pereira during the 1950s. *BPP, Medellin*

The magic of the radio will last a long time. Still, TV – you can not detract from its merits because it has given cycling a special tint, it has reached a broader audience and the images sell a lot. So TV is also important.

***How is the route of the Vuelta chosen each year?***

Economics has a lot to do with it. This year's circuit is good because it is passes through the mountains and most Colombian cyclists are lovers of mountain races. But that's luck. Towns pay for the Vuelta to pass through them. I am a mayor and I want to get the Vuelta to come to my city so I can show it. It's good for the hotel industry, for tourism and has many positive side effects.

***So it's just about the cycling?***

No. The Tour of Colombia is also a tour of the country and the history they taught us in school. About independence, for example. Most Colombians have not stood where Bolívar stood, where the battle of Boyacá was, or visited Bogota, where the cry for independence broke out.

Right here in Santander, there was the rebellion of the comuneros against Spain in 1781. We talk about these things as we cycle through the historic sites and bring them to our listeners all over the country.

We're not sure what's going on here! Alvaro Muñoz interviews the champion Ramón Hoyos in 1958.
*Biblioteca Publica Piloto, Medellin*

Similarly, with culture and cooking. There are very different traditions across Colombia. Valle del Cauca is different from Boyacá, which is different from Bogotá and Santander. We explain what we are experiencing as we follow the races. Not to all 50 million inhabitants but maybe half of them. We convey what we are seeing and the audience can enjoy it at a distance. We always include a story to illustrate the good things in life, especially to young people, who let themselves be carried away by modernism. Modernism is leading young people not to enjoy the simple things in life. From a fireplace, from a barbecue on charcoal, simple things that you enjoy. Those are the things that enrich us. These are the simple messages that accompany our broadcasts.

El Tiempo article explaining to readers how they could now watch the Vuelta on TV.
*El Tiempo*

# The 1980 Vuelta: Ringing the changes

The first five stages of the Vuelta featured five different winners. El Niño, Flórez and Cochise were all in the race but were well out of the lead.

Then on the 6th stage from Armenia to Buga, "the normal order was restored." El Niño won the stage with a brilliant display of strength. Flórez was just a few seconds behind him. José Patrocinio Jiménez was still in the overall lead.

1980 Vuelta a Colombia *Photo Jaimar*

Two stages later, el Niño took the leader's tricolour jersey, and held it to the end. But it was close: Flórez was on his tail, never more than 11 seconds behind but just unable to close the gap.

It was to be el Niño's last and sixth win in the Vuelta, a record which remains

Niño with his children at the end of his racing career. In the next decade he became a coach and one of the driving forces behind the Great Adventure. *Biblioteca Publica Piloto, Medellin*

unbroken. Although he continued trying looking for number seven, for some years.

It was also Cochise's last stage win. He had celebrated his 38th birthday on the eve of the Vuelta. He won the 10th stage by 90 seconds, giving him a record 39 stage wins over 19 years – and surpassing Hoyos' 38. It is another record which still stands and seems unlikely to be broken.

As we shall see, Alfonso Flórez had a lot more in the tank, and went on to win the Vuelta one more time, in 1983.

Meanwhile, the Seventies had drawn to a close. The old guard were hanging up their bikes and their boots. But as always, the slopes of the Cordillera Oriental had been busy nurturing new children, who would become famous far beyond Colombia.

One of them was a 20 year old called Fabio Parra, who won the Novices race in the Vuelta that year. The other was a skinny youth from Fusagasuga called Luis Herrera. His tenacity soon earned him the nickname 'Lucho', the Fighter.

Lucho Herrera will soon be famous *BPP, Medellin*

# 1980 Changing ends

Flórez chatting to gendarmes and spectators in France (c. 1980) *BPP, Medellin*

By 1980, teams of foreign riders had been coming to Colombia to compete in the Vuelta for almost 30 years. Spanish and Mexican riders were the most regular, but almost every Spanish speaking country of Latin America had visited, as well as Belgians, Czechs and the Swiss. Most of the Europeans had better equipment and a more disciplined approach to training, at least until el Niño came back from his European trip in 1973, full of new ideas.

Despite these advantages, no Latin American – other than a Colombian – had won the Vuelta a Colombia during that time. And only two Europeans, José Beyaert, and the Spaniard, José Gómez del Moral, had done so.

The Europeans had good excuses: the altitude, the length of the climbs, the food upsetting their stomachs. The accommodation was not what they were used to, either.

Soccer and rugby teams change ends at half time, in order to redress the natural advantages of one end over the other, whether it be the slope, the wind, or just the supporters.

During the past 15 years, Colombians had done some of that with their neighbours. They had been out and ridden all over Latin America: in Mexico, in Venezuela, in Argentina, Guatemala and Panama. Led by the giant figure of Cochise and Alvaro Pachon, they had done very well, both on the track and on the road.

Colombian national team in France c. 1981 (Patrocinio Jiménez in King of the Mountains jersey) *Biblioteca Publica Piloto, Medellin*

# The magic potions of the escarabajo

If you go to a cycle event in Colombia, you will find cyclists down at the start, busily carbing up on something that comes in little square packets. It looks like quince jelly, and that's not far wrong. It's *bocadillo*, a rubbery substance made by boiling up pulped guava fruit with sugar, and letting it set. Bocadillo is delicious and loaded with energy. If you need a caffeine rush, you can get bocadillo with crushed coffee beans, just like your caffeinated gels.

There may be street vendors at the start, dispensing liquid into the bidons and cups of the riders. Some is clearly hot, some cold but it doesn't look like pure water. It isn't, it's Agua Panela – a solution of *panela* dissolved in water, which is Colombia's national drink[19] although the rum is good as well. So what is panela?

Panela is unrefined cane sugar, which is set into cakes. You will find some version of panela in any country with a lot of cane (in India and East Africa, it is called jaggery). Panela is a high carb, concentrated food which provides an ideal source of energy to the cyclist. Dissolved in water, and spiced with herbs (lemon grass, mint or camomile, for example) it becomes the original hi-energy drink. It can be drunk hot or cold.

19. Coffee is an important export, but Colombians are not on the whole coffee aficionados. In fact, finding a decent coffee can be a struggle outside the main cities.

When they first arrived in 1980, the Colombian cyclists had never heard of gels. Flórez, Herrera, Jiménez and Co naturally took bocadillo and panela with them.

Pablo Wilches celebrates the extraordinary power of panela to revive and refresh, starting with Patrocinio Jiménez on the 1985 Vuelta a España.

The Europeans were suspicious at first. Were these strange substances the basis of their phenomenal climbing speeds? Were they legal or perhaps contained stimulants which should be banned from honest competition? After some investigation, the matter was cleared up to everyone's satisfaction.

European cyclists agonise over what to have for breakfast, before a big ride. Opinions are divided between the minimalist camp (fruit, coffee and yoghurt) and those who want to carb up with slow release muesli.

In Colombia, cuisine varies by region, and 70 years ago, when the Vuelta started, these variations were more marked.

For the Paisas (Antioquians), straddling the Central Cordillera, an important component of most meals was and is the *arepa*. An arepa is like a tortilla or pancake, but made from maize flour or pounded corn, mixed with butter and salt. Arepas are a great source of carbs.

Arepas are not exclusively Antioquian – you will find arepas stalls and street sellers all over Colombia and Venezuela – and even in New York!

An Arepa stall in Manhattan, Aug 2018 *Copyright: Author.*

But just as the Neapolitans know that they are the home of true pizza (and so do the Romans and the Argentines), the Antioquians know that they are the home of the real arepa. Arepas used to be eaten like bread, pita or chappati, on the side, but nowadays you can buy them stuffed with different fillings, and you can get sweeter ones for breakfast.

next left page

# 1980 Changing ends

But the Colombians had not 'changed ends' with the Europeans; they had not sent a proper team to Europe. Cochise had ridden in one Tour de France, as a domestique.

This was about to change.
It started in 1980, when the organizers of the Tour de l'Avenir – in those days, the amateur equivalent of the Tour de France but nowadays a novice race – invited Colombia to send a team.

To the amazed joy of the entire nation, Alfonso Flórez defeated the Russian Sergey Sukhoruchenkov. "Suku" had won the race the two previous years, and was the reigning Olympic road racing champion. Flórez showed true grit throughout the 12 days of the contest. He struggled on the flat, but managed to hold on to early gains on the mountains until the finish line.

It was a fantastic achievement, but it was only the beginning of "the second half." The next year, 1981, saw an epic ride by the Colombians, in which 3 riders finished in the top 10, and Patrocinio Jiménez came $3^{rd}$ and won the King of the Mountains.

Even better was to come, when in 1983, the Tour de France was opened to amateurs and Colombia was invited to send a team.

Curious stares from stall holders as cyclist races through. *Biblioteca Publica Piloto, Medellin*

Tour de l'Avenir, 1981. A huge triumph: the podium at the end of the Tour de l'Avenir: Pascal Simon (FRA), Sergei Soukhoruchenkov $2^{nd}$ and Patrocinio Jiménez $3^{rd}$ and King of the Mountains. *Biblioteca Publica Piloto, Medellin*

# The magic potions of the escarabajo

from previous left page

So it is not surprising to find Ramón Hoyos – on winning his first Vuelta – being feted by an Antioquian cowboy who hung a giant arepa around his neck, to show that he is a real paisa. And in 2002, José Castelblanco was likewise garlanded with a necklace of arepas after winning the Vuelta (see photo)

In Medellin, a cyclist will consume several arepas for breakfast, and tuck another away for the ride. He or she will NOT, if they have any discretion, breakfast on another traditional dish of the region, the **Bandeja Paisa** (the "Paisa Platter"), which is a vast pile of rice, red beans, sausages (chorizos), pork, chicken and black pudding (morcilla), topped with a fried egg, avocado and maybe a fried plantain. And an arepa or two for good measure. All served on a huge platter. After you have ridden over the Alto de Minas to La Pintada and back, you will be ready for this, but not before.

Vuelta a Colombia, Bogota 27th Jan 2002 José Castelblanco feted with a necklace of arepas. *Foto Hernán Vanegas*

On the eastern side of the Magdalena River, the rivals of Antioquia, that is to say the cyclists of Boyacá, Santander and Cundinamarca, not to mention the capital, might start the day with *changua*. A classic *changua* consists of an egg or two, lightly poached in a soup which is half water, half milk, with a dash of salt. The soup is served with scallions, cilantro and special stale bread.

# Stranger in a strange land

The Colombian team stood out among the Europeans, and were not always welcome. Patrocinio Jiménez remembers:

*"Well, yes, we were weird because we got there with our wool shorts, our wool shirts, our arepas, our panela...we just wanted to participate. Some assholes in the German team made fun of us in the dining room: they covered their mouths with their hands and howled like in the cowboy movies. As if we were the bad Indians of the movie. But a team from Switzerland gave us Lycra uniforms and another offered us an energy drink. [That was] when the panela was finished. Then the announcers and journalists began to tell the story that our secret recipe was panela. But that was back in the 80s."*

It was not easy for a Colombian to ride in Europe in the 1980s, with strange food, strange clothes and strange customs.

Europe was an unfamiliar world to the Colombian riders.
*Biblioteca Publica Piloto, Medellin*

1981

# The 1981 Vuelta a Colombia

The 1981 Vuelta was a bad tempered affair which presaged some of the troubles to come.

Flórez was back from his extraordinary victory in Europe, and hungry for more when the 31st Vuelta kicked off in Cucuta on 16th June, 1981. Too hungry, perhaps.

On the 8th stage from Bogota to Honda, he fell and despite urgent and repeated attention from his support team, he was unable to continue. Later the organisers announced that he was in any case disqualified for failing a drugs test he had taken that morning.

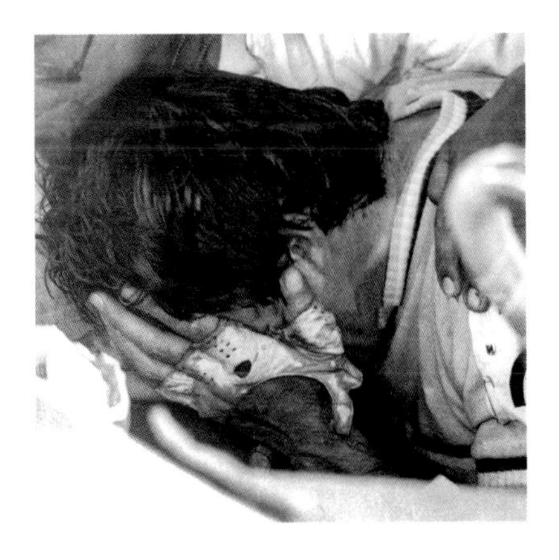

Vuelta 1980: Alfonso Flórez retires but is later disqualified for failing a drugs test. Horacio Gil Ochoa took this photo and said later:
*"He didn't show his face, neither when he got off the bike nor in the car. I swear that I was sorry to take photos. But he was news."*
*Biblioteca Publica Piloto, Medellin*

Ossitto Cycling team was sanctioned for the bear distributing marijuana to spectators
*Biblioteca Publica Piloto, Medellin*

Drugs in all forms were grabbing the headlines. A member of the Bicicletas Ositto team – owned by Roberto Escobar, Pablo's brother – was expelled from the race for giving away marijuana to his fellow travellers.

Cochise, now a trainer, had a new star pupil, Epifanio Arcila, who led the race for 8 stages.

But el Niño was still riding hard and he had a new teammate in the Loteria de Boyacá team, a 21 year old named Fabio Parra. The pair attacked on June 24th as the race went over the traditional monster climb of Letras.

Fabio Parra won the stage by 38 seconds, el Niño was 3 minutes behind. A complaint was made to the stewards that the race leader, Epifanio Arcila, had been assisted with a push from his coach Cochise, but this was denied. Arcila was still almost 4 minutes ahead overall.

Two days later, Niño and Parra arrived together in Medellin over Minas, three minutes ahead of Arcila. Arcila was still wearing the jersey, but now Parra was just 29 seconds behind.

The next day was one of the toughest stages of the race (see the altimetria below, taken from the *El Tiempo* newspaper that morning). It started from Caldas, a small town just south of Medellin, and went south over the Alto de Minas. From here the riders made the long, dangerous descent of 2,000 metres

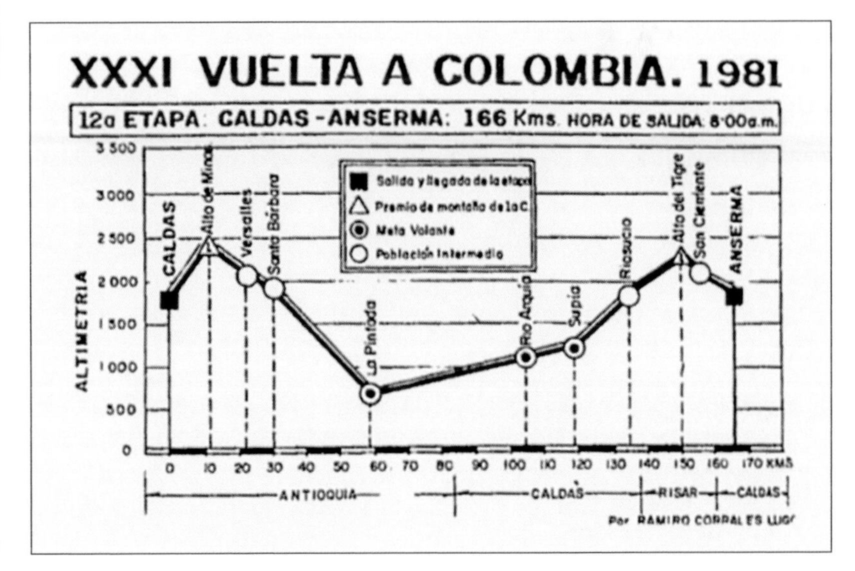


Altimetría from El Tiempo showing the route of the 12th stage of the 1981 Vuelta in which Fabio Parra took the jersey. *Copyright: El Tiempo 28 June 1981*

Acevedo Porras wins stage 12 into Anserma during the 1981 Vuelta. Behind him, Fabio Parra gained enough time on Epifanio Arcila to take the leaders jersey.
*Biblioteca Publica Piloto, Medellin*

1981

# The 1981 Vuelta a Colombia

1981 Vuelta a Colombia: Patrocinio Jiménez (No 89) leads the peleton. *Photo Humberto Arango*

to La Pintada and then climbed again over the Alto de Tigre before finishing in the mountain town of Anserma.

Look at the profile of the race on the altimetría on the previous page. You can see why Lucho Herrera thought the Alpine climbs were too short. It is 90 kilometres uphill from the river to the Alto de Tigre!

Parra and Arcila went over the first climb together, but Parra outbraked Arcila on the descent and arrived at La Pintada 40 seconds ahead.

On the long climb, Fabio Parra gained on Arcila with every pedal stroke, arriving at the top 4 minutes ahead, and taking another 30 seconds on the downhill into Anserma.

"I have prepared for this for over a year," said the 21 year old Parra from the stage podium that afternoon, "and I am sure that I am going to win it. Nothing can stop me."

He was right. The Loteria Boyacá team, led by el Niño and Parra, rode a tight formation over the remaining stages. In the end Parra rode into Cali to win the Vuelta by 75 seconds over his closest rival. Arcila came in 3rd, el Niño 4th.

Aged 21, the future looked bright for Parra. Among the crowd of young finishers, there was no particular reason to worry about an even younger talent, one Luis Alberto Herrera, who had just turned 20 and came third in the novices race, 38 minutes behind.

That was going to change any day now.

1981 Vuelta. Crowds watch the cyclists arrive (see the bunch heading away to finish)
*Biblioteca Publica Piloto, Medellin*

# The little bear of the Escobars

The best known – if not the most successful – drug fuelled cycling enterprise was Bicicletas Ositto. Bicicletas Ositto was a bike maker of sorts owned by Pablo Escobar's older brother Roberto 'Osito' ('little bear').

A cyclist himself in the 1960s, he had once arrived at the finish of a race in Medellin plastered in mud. "I don't know who this is," said the race commentator, "his race number and his face are so covered in mud, he looks more like a bear." So he was known as Osito, the little bear, ever after (he called his company Ositto with a double t because he thought it had an Italian flavour and Italian bikes were cool).

Roberto Escobar (left) was a team-mate of Cochise's. He competed abroad and rode in the Vuelta twice. *BPP, Medellin*

Roberto was a serious cyclist in his own right. As a child, he had an old touring bike which he painted with his fingers because he loved it and had no paintbrush. He used to carry his little brother Pablo on the handlebars. One afternoon in 1958, he and Pablo climbed the Alto de Minas and watched Fausto Coppi and Hugo Koblet go by, on their way to humiliation by Hoyos and Medina in the heat of La Pintada and the slopes of the Alto de Minas. That was the afternoon his heart was set on becoming a real cyclist.

And he succeeded. He had ridden in the Vuelta and the RCN and had several stage wins to his name. He trained in the Antioquian team alongside Cochise.
In 1965, aged 18, he and Cochise took part in the 100 kilometres team time trial in the National Cycling championships, and he came third. That same year, he rode in the Vuelta a Colombia and finished 38th. In 1966, he rode again and finished a creditable 32nd.

Pablo and Roberto continued their interest in cycling after Roberto retired from racing. Pablo bought the building which became Bicicletas Ositto's cycle factory.

Horacio Gil Ochoa's image of the entrance to Pablo Escobar's ranch. *Biblioteca Publica Piloto, Medellin*

Visitors to the facility were surprised to find a modest workshop rather than a production line. But still, in 1980, Ositto entered its first team for the Vuelta a Colombia. The bikes were proudly labelled "Ositto" but the frames were actually made by José Duarte, Colombia's premier frame maker. According to Duarte, Pablo himself used to visit the frame maker's shop in Bogota in person, to check up on progress.

Pablo Escobar was not the right shape for cycling himself. His love was fast cars, and during the late 1970s and 1980s he raced competitively.

next left page

# 1982 The tortoise beat the hares

Fabio Parra and Luis Herrera were two of the youngest riders waiting in the main square of Tunja for the start of the 1982 Vuelta. They were surrounded not only by the cream of Colombian cycling but also a bevy of European riders, including Pascal Simon, winner of the Tour de l'Avenir the year before.

Parra was 22, Herrera 21, but they must have felt their time had come. As just discussed, Parra had won the Vuelta the year before. And seven weeks prior, the pair had fought each other in the Clásico RCN[4].

The precocious Herrera had come from behind in the RCN with a spectacular performance in the last two days of climbing. Parra was subcampeon[5] . They had defeated not only the cream of domestic completion but also two top class foreigners, the Frenchman Pascal Simon and the Scot Robert Millar.

Herrera got off to a good start in the 1982 Vuelta. On the 3rd stage, he went over the Alto de Letras first, taking the lead in the King of the Mountains, although on the descent he was overtaken by more experienced riders.

Fashionable ladies watching the Vuelta a Colombia. *Biblioteca Publica Piloto, Medellin*

But the Stage of Death was waiting for him. Descending from the Alto de Minas, he had a bad fall and had to abandon the race.

This should have been good news for Parra. He tagged along, staying in touch but without winning a stage or taking the lead. After being runner-up to Herrera in the Clásico RCN, he had been training in France, and came home to defend his Vuelta title.

Ambulance, dog and curious spectators. *Biblioteca Publica Piloto, Medellin*

But he was tired and struggled to stay with the leaders throughout the race. On the last stage, the big climb from Honda up to Bogota, he hoped to win big and take the title. But instead he faded and lost time, and wound up 9th in the General Classification, with el Niño in 10th and Alfonso Flórez right behind him.

4. The RCN had started off as a 2 day event back in 1961, but by 1982 it was a tough 10 days on the road, and was becoming as prestigious as the Vuelta.

5. In English, "second" has negative connotations, as in "second hand" and "second best." Spanish uses the glass half-full term, "subcampeon," which I prefer.

# The little bear of the Escobars

Pablo Escobar started racing souped up Renault 4s, but graduated to BMWs and then to a Porche 935. His car racing and his brother Robert's cycling team were all under the Ossitto banner, as you can see from the windshield.
*Photo El Colombiano*

from previous left page

But he was a genuine aficionado of cycling. He and Roberto used to ride around on a Vespa scooter, supporting their team, or by helicopter if the stage was too far away.

Pablo had a private velodrome built just above El Poblado, a suburb of Medellin. Roberto would assemble teams of top quality Colombian cyclists to race round it. And bet huge sums on the outcome, of course.

By all accounts, the drug lords in the 1970s and early 1980s were socially respectable. They did not advertise or even consider themselves to be criminals. They were just rich, smart Colombians whose generosity made them welcome wherever they chose to spend their money.

As we know now, it didn't last. Indeed it ended with appalling violence and the murder of thousands of innocent (and many less innocent) people.

Roberto was captured by the police in 1992 and charged with multiple offences including possession of weapons, drug trafficking, kidnapping, extortion, accessory to murder and escaping from a maximum security prison (not exactly maximum security –he and Pablo had famously walked out of the Envigado prison which Pablo had created for his negotiated incarceration).

In 1993, (by now back in prison) Roberto was partially blinded by a letter bomb, just 17 days after Pablo Escobar was killed by the security forces.

Today he lives with his bodyguards and supplements his income by entertaining tourists.

Roberto Escobar, el Osito, today. *Photo Donaldo Zuluaga*

# The tortoise beat the hares

Luis Herrera feted after winning the 1982 Clásico RCN. *Photo Hernando Vasquez*

So if Parra, Herrera, el Niño and Flórez were all out of it, who won the 1982 Vuelta? The answer is 30 year old Cristobal Perez, who achieved GC victory without winning a single stage along the way. Perez was a trooper. He had been road racing for almost a decade with solid but unspectacular success. He had represented Colombia in the team time trial at the Olympics in 1976. He was no slouch – he came third in the Tour de l'Avenir the same year.

Dispirited, Parra quit cycling.

What does he say about it today?

*"I rode for the love of the shirt, for love of the sport…if there was any money, it was very little. And it was a very hard life. And I said to myself, what am I going to live on later?"*

So he parked his bike and, like the "Student Prince" Hernán Medina a decade before, went to college instead. Not for long, as it turned out.

It wasn't a great year either for Flórez. He arrived in 10th place (he had been allowed back after testing positive for drugs in 1981). And Rafael Niño wasn't happy with his 11th place. The great man announced that he was "hanging up" his bike and would not be back. Well, not as a rider. Like Cochise, he became a coach. Actually, he became THE coach of the exciting national team of the 1980s and he continues to manage a Colombian team to this day.

Mending punctures in the rain. *BPP, Medellin*

Horacio Gil Ochoa, cycling aficionado, photographer and author of the photographic homage to Colombian cycling, *"Mi bicicleta, mi camara y yo"*.

# The lens of Ochoa

Horacio Gil (pronounced Heel with a guttural 'h') Ochoa was born in Barbosa, Antioquia in 1930. For almost 40 years, he photographed cycling races. Not just the riders, but the officials, the scenery and the spectators. His photos evoke the full gamut of emotions in this toughest of sports: the nervousness before the start, the pain of the ride, triumph and despair at the finish.

It wasn't an easy living. His son Juan remembers how his father would spend the day taking pictures, then race back to Medellin, to develop them in time to be printed in the next morning's newspapers.

His favourite event was the Vuelta a Colombia, but he went to as many races as he could, in Colombia, Mexico, Guatamala and also to Europe with the Colombian team.

One of his favourite spots was the ford at Supia, featured on the front cover of this book. Another was the "Curve of the Violin," which he would photograph every year when the racing went that way. (Photo 1)

He didn't like accidents and unlike some of his contemporaries, didn't hang around big ruts in the road waiting for the next crash. But inevitably he saw a fair number, and had to record them, including this, one of his most famous. (Photo 2)

He loved people. Many photos convey his concern for dangers of the sport, and those who worried about those risks. (Photo 3)

He could be funny, like this: (Photo 4)

And when we view this image, we share the wonderment of the spectator and the sweat of the rider: (Photo 5)

He died in 2018 in his city of Medellin, a much revered figure. He left behind 350,000 negatives to the Medellin Biblioteca Publica Piloto, of which only a tiny handful are reproduced in this book.

If you have a head for heights, the Curve of the Violin is a great place to watch the race go by. *Biblioteca Publica Piloto, Medellin*

2

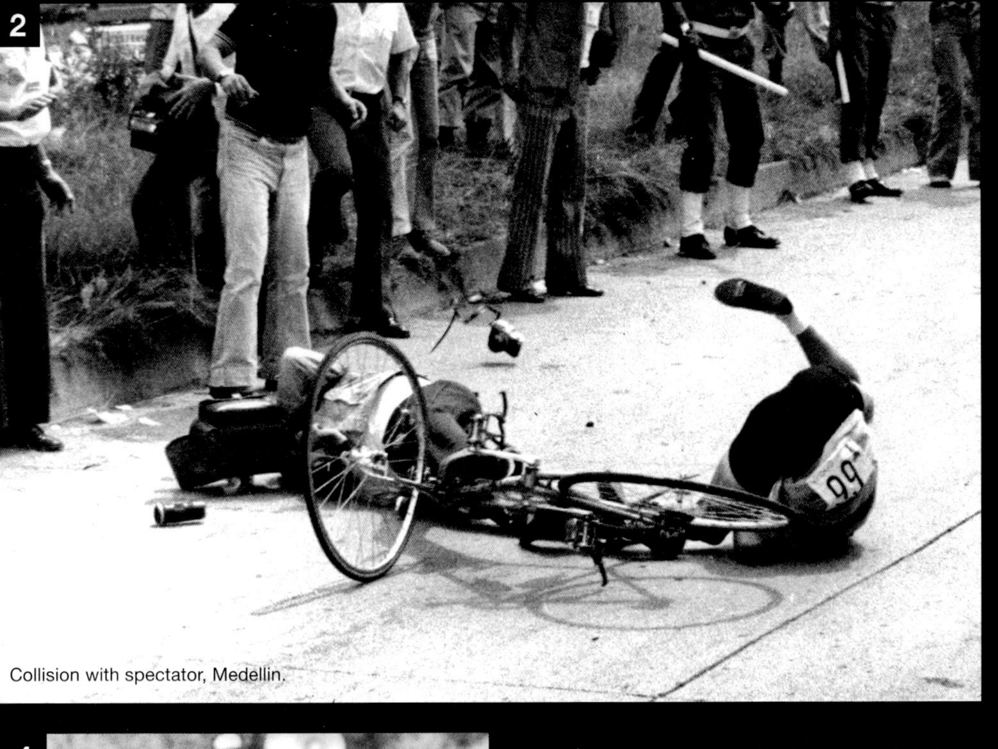

Collision with spectator, Medellin.

3

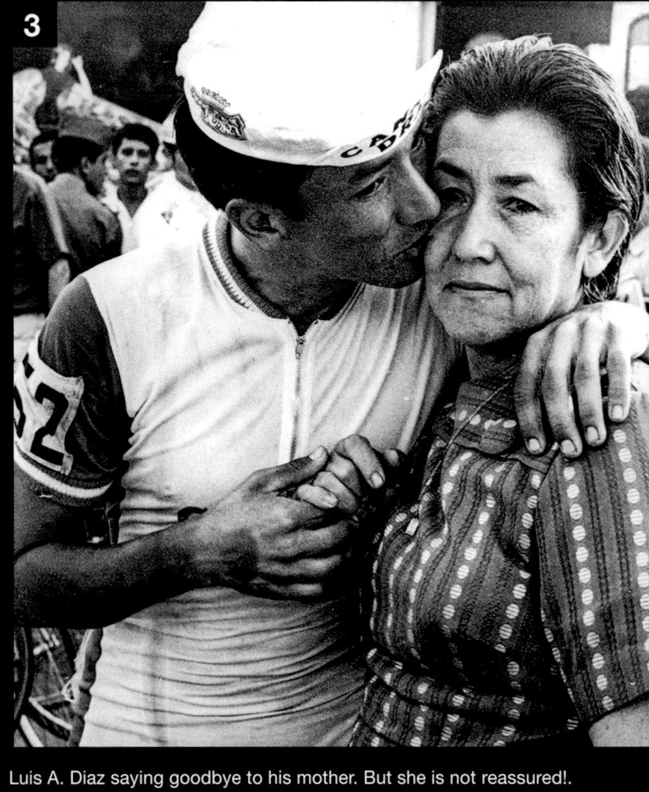

Luis A. Diaz saying goodbye to his mother. But she is not reassured!.

All pictures © *Biblioteca Publica Piloto, Medellin*

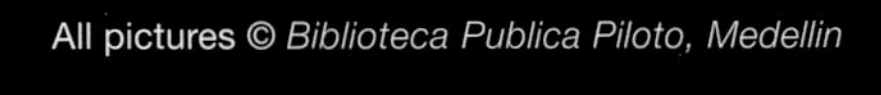

4

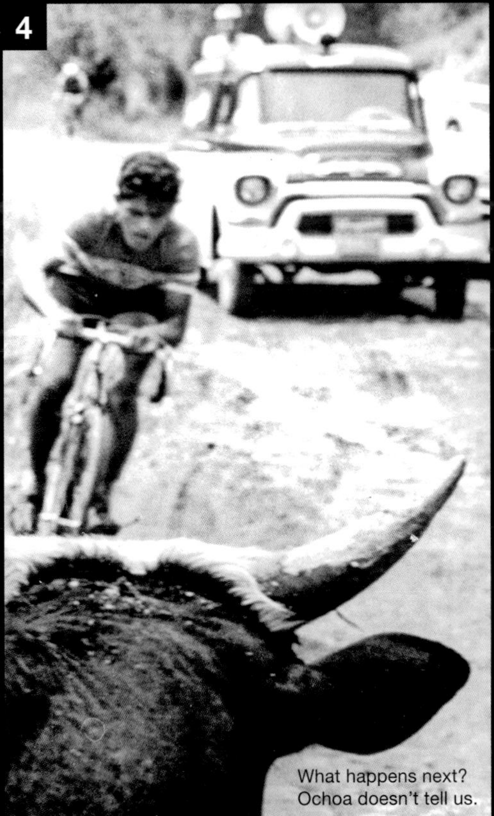

What happens next? Ochoa doesn't tell us.

5

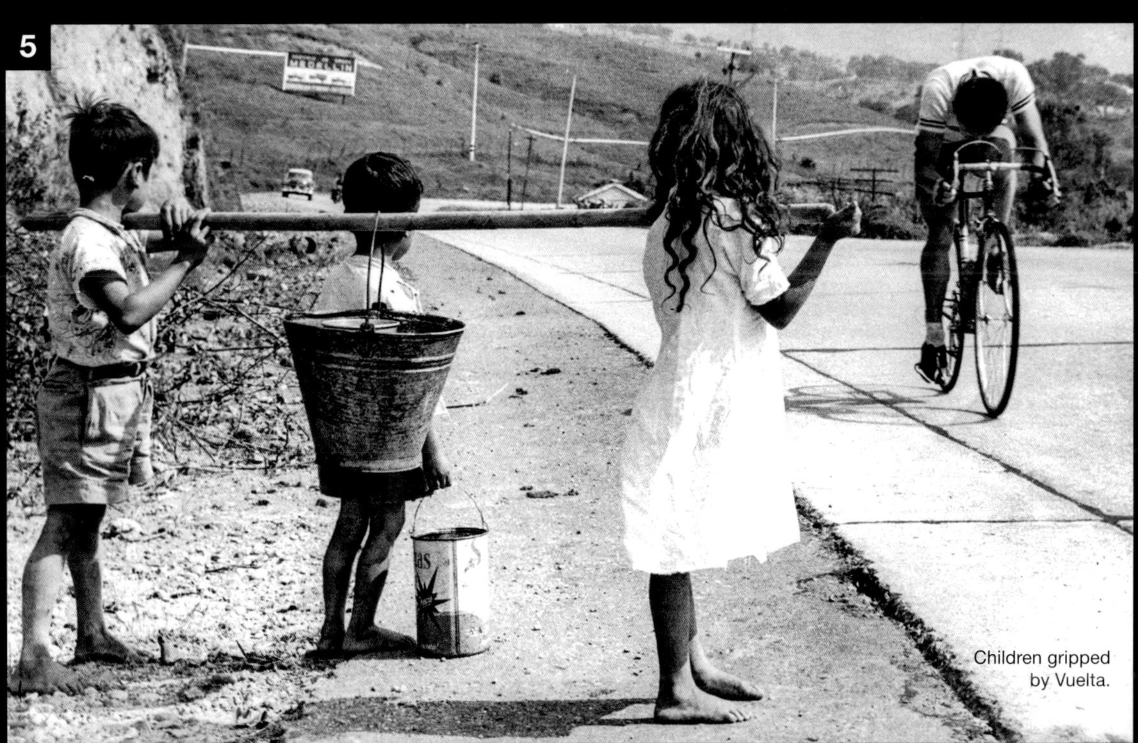

Children gripped by Vuelta.

# Alfonso Flórez Ortiz

## Born
5th November, 1952
Bucaramanga
Altitude 959 metres

## Early days
Alfonso Flórez was an only son but with 4 sisters. He wanted to be an athlete but gave up athletics after a disappointing race. Then he tried soccer but gave that up also. He was not committed to anything, until two things happened: he won a touring bike in a raffle, and he fell in love. He was a passionate cyclist and suitor (but struggled to convince his fiancee's father because of a philandering reputation). But he eventually succeeded in both, marrying Marta Tarazona and getting a place in the Postobon team in Medellin.

## Career
He won two stages of the Vuelta a Colombia on his debut, 1974, and moved up. He was 3rd in GC in 1977 and 2nd in 1978. In 1979, he won the Vuelta a Colombia for the first time, controversially against team orders. His eldest daughter was born a week or two later. Then he led the national (Varta) team to France and became the first Colombian to win the Tour de l'Avenir. After that he cycled with the Café de Colombia/Varta team in Europe until 1987. In 1983 he won the Vuelta a Colombia for a second time.

## Vuelta a Colombia podium
1979, 1983.

## Later days
A popular figure in Medellin, he did not go on to become a coach or manager after retiring. He was assassinated on 27th April, 1992 and his death was never fully explained. One possibility is that he was having an affair with the wife or girlfriend of a narco-trafficker, who didn't appreciate it.

## Grand Tour & Other wins
None, but he won the Tour de l'Avenir in 1980 and finished the Tour de France twice.

## Vuelta a Colombia stages: 6

# 1983 Europe beckons

1983 was an exciting year for Colombian cycling aficionados. The organisers of the Tour de France opened the race to amateurs, hoping to attract some Eastern European teams. Instead they got Colombians. With great difficulty, the President of the Colombian Cycling Federation, Miguel Angel Bermudez, found the money needed to fund the squad (from the Colombian division of Varta Batteries), and appointed Cochise and Rubén Darío Gómez as joint team directors.

Fabio Parra cooling himself. *BPP, Medellin*

The natural choice of a rider to lead the Colombian team was Alfonso Flórez. Everyone remembered that he had won the Tour de l'Avenir three years back.

His co-leader was Patrocinio Jiménez. The rest consisted of the finest riders in the country – although not Herrera and Parra, who were considered too young and unproven to be in it. Parra in any case was back in college, at least for the moment.

Champions in the making. The team that became the engine of Colombian success in Europe in the 1980s seen here digging deep in the 1981 Vuelta a Antioquia: Samuel Cabrera, Abelardo Rios, Martín Ramírez, Tomate Agudelo, Patrocinio Jiménez. *Photo José Betancur*

# La Wilchería: the amazing Wilches brothers

Team Wilches in 2017, with Pablo as technical director.
3 generations of Wilches have raced professionally in Colombia.
*Facebook*

The name Wilches is appears frequently in Colombian cycling records. That's because there were a lot of them – and they were good. Pablo Wilches and his 3 brothers came from the cycling town of Fusagasuga, home of many distinguished riders including Lucho Herrera.

Pablo rode in the Dauphiné in 1984 and finished 5th. In 1985 he rode in the national team supporting Herrera and Parra.

In 1987 he entered the Vuelta a Colombia, riding with his three younger brothers: Ricardo, Gustavo and Marcos. These three were just amateurs and they were up against the might of the national squad, including Herrera, Flórez and Jiménez. Amazingly the Wilches vanquished them all. Pablo Wilches won the GC, and Gustavo came third, with Herrera between them.

And that was just the beginning! In 1990, Gustavo won the Vuelta a Colombia and the Clásico RCN. Pablo was 4th in the Vuelta and 3rd in the Clásico RCN.

A year later, Pablo was first past the post both in the Vuelta and the Clásico RCN, beating not only his younger brother, but a strong field of young talent. Alas, traces of nandrolone – a popular but banned steroid – were found in his bloodstream and he was disqualified from both competitions.

The Wilches family continued an on-off relationship with drugs. Ricardo was caught drug smuggling in Mexico in 2000 and given a long gaol term. Gustavo was arrested at Bogota Airport in 2001. X-rays revealed 40 packets of heroin in his stomach. A year later, the youngest brother, Marcos, was shot dead by two unknown gunmen who were trying to steal his taxi.

But the dynasty survived! Two of Pablo's sons became professional cyclists, and rode internationally. In 2016, the family announced the creation of "Team Wilches" with Pablo as technical director. This team of 16 Elite riders includes three Wilches from the next generation, and behind them, there are no less than eight Wilches descendants in the pre-juvenile category!

Pablo Wilches and his 3 brothers founded a cycling dynasty.
*Biblioteca Publica Piloto, Medellin*

## Tant pis!

The 1983 Colombian team made history when they were sanctioned at the start of the first stage, for this:
"We arrived at the start line and seeing the great men of the Tour de France like Bernard Hinault, Laurent Fignon, Greg Lemond, "Perico" Delgado, Stephen Roche and Sean Kelly, it scared us and our nerves got the better of us, we urinated everywhere, as we did in Colombia ...
In the afternoon, in the official bulletin, the Colombian team was sanctioned.
"The whole team", it said, "for urinating."

## 1983

# Europe beckons

By a happy accident, the Vuelta a Colombia was due to start 4 weeks before the Tour de France. So the new Colombian national team signed up for it, under the Varta banner, and a number of French national riders, looking for high altitude training, came to join the Vuelta.

While the team was In Colombia, things went well. “Varta A Nacional” had discipline and they were well drilled. Flórez took the jersey on the 4th stage and held it to the end. It was his second Vuelta victory.

Then the team left for France, along with high expectations and over 30 reporters! And so the Great Adventure – as the press dubbed it – began.

Flórez and his team arrived a few weeks later in France.

Flórez himself was defeated by the first 1,600 kilometres of flat roads, cobblestones and wind. To a Colombian, the 300 dull kilometres from Roubaix to Le Havre (to pick just one example) was a day in Purgatory, painful and pointless.

The VARTA A national squad in full song during the Vuelta a Colombia June 1983. Patrocinio Jiménez is cooling his team leader, Alfonso Flórez. *Photo Hernando Vasquez*

But his teammate Patrocinio Jiménez struggled through to the Alps and spent five days in the King of the Mountains jersey. It was a great achievement, the first time that any Colombian had ever worn the Tour de France polka dots, even for a night. The celebrations back home in Bogota went on all night.

Alfonso Flórez celebrates his second Vuelta a Colombia win before heading off to lead the Colombian team in their first Tour de France. *Photo Hernando Vasquez*

# Aficionados and drug lords

By 1980, **cocaine** had become Colombia's major export and source of foreign currency. It had brought **enormous wealth**, especially to Antioquia and its capital **Medellin.** The drug lords had more money than Croesius and needed **entertaining.** And like the rest of Colombia, they had been brought up on the **Vuelta**, the RCN Clásico and the glory of road racing. So they were **cycling fans.**

**Sponsoring** a cycling team was a cool thing to do with your money. Of course, you needed a **business** to be the official sponsor of your team. Conveniently, the drug lords already owned businesses which they used for **laundering** the cash they made from selling cocaine[6].

In 1985, a chain of **jewellery stores**, Joyerias Felipe, **sponsored** a team with stunning **success** in the Vuelta a Colombia. They had four riders in the top ten of the General Classification, and won 2nd place in the KOM competition. The owner of Joyerias Felipe was Rodrigo Murillo Pardo, a senior player in the **Medellin cartel**. Alas, the successes of the Joyerias Felipe team came to an abrupt **end** when Pardo was **murdered** by his Medellin associates in 1986.

Another **cocaine-powered** enterprise was Drogueria Yaneth – a pharmacy chain – and its sibling business Parfumeria Yaneth. These enterprises were owned by José Gilberto Rodríguez Gacha, **"the Mexican."** Gacha was Colombian from Cundinamarca but he had a passion for all things Mexican and was credited with developing **US trafficking** routes using the Mexican cartels. He also created a well-trained and well-armed **private army** for the Medellin cartel.

**Drogueria Yaneth** was not short of funds, and in 1980 it sponsored three teams with considerable **success.** For a start, el Niño had been riding for Drogueria Yaneth A when he won the 1980 Vuelta.

On December 15, 1989, the **Mexican** and his son Freddy were **killed** in a dramatic **shootout** on the **Caribbean** coast with two helicopters carrying an elite Colombian **police** squad. That was the **end** of the Drogueria Yaneth teams.

But the greatest and most notorious **link** between **cycling** and **cocaine** was forged by the **Escobar brothers**, Pablo and Roberto (see insert). They had been cycling **fans** since **childhood**, and Roberto was a serious and **successful cyclist** in his own right, who rode with Cochise in the 1960s and 70s. The Escobars didn't just sponsor a team, they built a private **velodrome** in Medellin and started a **bicycle manufacturing** business.

But by all accounts, the **drug lords** in the 1970s and early 1980s were socially **respectable.** They did not advertise or consider themselves to be evil gangsters. They were just **rich**, smart Colombians whose generosity made them **welcome** wherever they chose to spend their money.

As we know now, it didn't last. Indeed it ended with appalling **violence** and the **murder** of **thousands** of innocent (and some less innocent) people. Among them were a number of distinguished **ex-riders** who were drawn into the narcotics trade and eventually became **victims** of it.

6. The cycling teams themselves were not significant to the laundering operations, they were just playthings of rich gangsters.

# 1984 Triumph of the little gardener

Luis Herrera was nicknamed "the little gardener of Fusagasuga" by the commentators. This epithet conveys in one package his slight stature, his hometown and his first job.

Over the next 5 years, he left gardening behind him and became the world's greatest climber. At home, he won the Vuelta a Colombia every year for the next five years, except for 1987, when he had to content himself with second place. He also won the Clásico RCN in 1982, 1983 and 1984 and 1986, and was second in 1985.

Colombian cycling in 1984 had talent in depth. Here we see Flórez (62), with Herrera behind (81), Parra (76). *Biblioteca Publica Piloto, Medellin*

During the 1980s, intenational cyclists discovered Colombia. Here a boyish Greg Lemond smilles at Horacio Gil Ochoa. *BPP, Medellin*

Back in his university, Fabio Parra was green with envy as he watched his old cycling buddies being hired by well-funded international teams and racing in Europe. In 1984, he could bear it no longer! He suspended his studies and returned to cycling. He signed up with Herrera's old sponsor, Leche el Gran Via, as did some of Lucho's old teammates.

The big European teams had by this time figured out the benefits of training at altitude, namely the natural increase in oxygen carrying red blood cells. Now that the Vuelta and the Clásico RCN were taking place earlier in the year, Colombia was the ideal place to start the season and boost those hematocrit levels legally.

So when the Clásico RCN set off in April, 1984, the field was awash with Colombian and foreign talent. Laurent Fignon, who was the reigning Tour de France champion, the American Greg Lemond and Bernard Hinault were all riding.

# Fabio Enrique Parra Pinto

## Born
22nd Nov 1959
Sogamosa
Altitude 2569

## Nickname
Parra – he never got a nickname!

## Early days
His father was a cyclist, but started too late to win big (he rode in the Vuelta a Colombia aged 29). But he passed on his enthusiasm to his sons. Fabio started cycling at aged 15 and won a succession of youth races. In 1979, aged 19, he won both the Vuelta a Juventidad & the novice section in the Vuelta a Colombia.

## Career
In 1980, Parra was 13th in GC, but 1981 he won Vuelta a Colombia outright. To his dismay, he did not win in 1982. So he quit cycling and went off college. He was drawn back when he saw his old rivals on TV, now competing in Europe. Riding for the national team Café de Colombia, he won the novice section of the Tour de France in 1985. In 1988, with the Spanish team Kelme, he was 3rd in GC at the Tour de France, and the following year, 1989, he was 2nd in the Vuelta a España, the first Colombian to have been on the podium in either. In 1992, aged 32, he won the Vuelta a Colombia for the second and last time.

## Vuelta a Colombia stages: 6

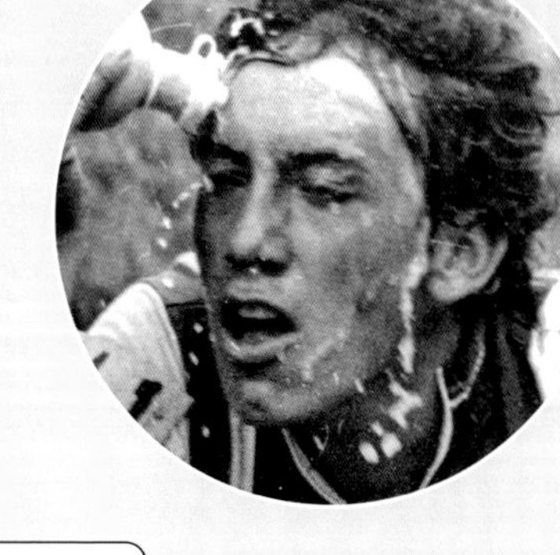

## Grand Tour & Other wins
3rd GC in Tour de France, 2nd GC in Vuelta a España. 7x Vuelta a España, always finishing in 8th place GC or higher. 8 starts in Tour de France, 4 finishes.

## Vuelta a Colombia podium
Won in 1981, 1992.
2nd in 1985, 1989 and 3rd in 1984.

## Later days
Parra hung up his bike in 1992. He had had two bad accidents. In 1991 in Spain, warming up for a time trial, he hit a trolley laden with cement and smashed his face. When he retired, he studied business administration, and set up a plastic packaging company. He has little connection with cycling nowadays – except that his company makes bidons – plastic cycling bottles.

1984

# Triumph of the little gardener

The Europeans were there to train, not to die in the attempt. Perhaps for that reason, they finished well down the field. Herrera won, and Parra, recently returned after his year off, was fifth. This was a good start.

The Vuelta a Colombia was next, in May 1984, and again Herrera trounced the opposition, winning both the GC and the King of the Mountains competition. Parra was third.

Lucho Herrera was no longer considered too young and inexperienced to ride abroad! A few weeks later, he led the Colombian National Team, sponsored by Varta, in the 1984 Tour de France. The race arrived at the Alps on Stage 17, which finished on the Alpe d'Huez.

On the final climb up to the Alpe d'Huez, Herrera rode away from Bernard Hinault and led up the 21 hairpins to the top. His victory over Hinault, Robert Millar, Laurent Fignon, not to mention Greg Lemond, was the first by a Colombian rider in any Grand Tour, and was celebrated with wild enthusiasm back home.

This short TV clip celebrates the international success of Lucho Herrera, beginning with his famous victory on the Alpe d'Huez.

"Herrera beat the superstars yesterday!" trumpeted El Tiempo, noting that the Colombian victory had been mentioned both by President Mitterand and – bizarrely – the US Democratic convention.

Bernard Hinault "the badger" in action c.1984. Hinault's aggressive style inspired fear and respect among the Colombians. *BPP, Medellin*

Carlos Maria Jaramillo and Rogelio Arango feel the heat. Just two of the talented domestiques who supported Parra and Herrera on the Great Adventure. *Biblioteca Publica Piloto, Medellin*

But it was not just Herrera. *There were no less than 6 Colombians in the first 20 riders that day.* His Varta team mates Rafael Acevedo and Alfonso Flórez were 5th and 11th, and Pablo Wilches, one of the four cycling Wilches brothers, was 9th, riding for a European team.

With this depth of talent, it seemed as though Colombian teams and Colombian riders were going to conquer the world, and that the world would flock to the Colombian corderillas to boost their red blood cells and expand their lungs.

## Luis Alberto Herrera Herrera

### Born
4th May, 1961
Fusagasugá,
Cundinamarca
Altitude 1,728 m

### Nickname
El Jardinerito
(the little gardener)

### Grand Tour & Other wins
Champion and KOM, Vuelta a España 1987, KOM Tour de France 1985, 1986, 1987, KOM Giro d'Italia 1989, 1990. Criterium du Dauphine Libere 1988, 1991.

### Early days
Lucho and his four brothers were brought up in the country near Fusagasugá, where their parents had a farm. His mother got him a bike to ride to school, 6 kilometres away. Legend has it that he worked as a gardener part time while in high school, and used the bike to get there. At any rate, he started competing with that bike. As with so many other aspiring escarabajos, he had a portable radio and listened, captivated, by the triumphs of Cochise, Pachon and others.

### Vuelta a Colombia stages: 7

### Career
He rode in his first Vuelta a Colombia in 1981 and finished 16th, 3rd in the Novices. In 1982, he won the Clásico RCN and 1983 the Clásico RCN again, and finished sub-campeon to Alfonso Flórez in the 1983 Vuelta a Colombia. He matured rapidly. 1984 was an astonishing year: he won the Vuelta a Colombia, the Clásico RCN and famously the Tour de France stage 17, a mountain finish up the Alpe d'Huez. He was the first Colombian to win a stage in the Tour, and the first amateur to do so in the history of the Tour.
He would go on to win the Vuelta a Colombia and the Clásico RCN four times each but his greatest achievement was in 1987, when he won the Vuelta a España, the first Latin American to win a Grand Tour. Herrera also won the Critérium du Dauphiné Libéré in 1988 and 1991 and five "King of the Mountains" jerseys from the three Grand Tours. He was also only the second rider to win the King of the Mountains jersey in all three Grand Tours.

### Vuelta a Colombia podium
GC winner in 1984, 1985, 1986 and 1988.
He also won the RCN Clásico 4 times.

### Later days
On Christmas eve 1991, he married a model and ex-beauty queen Judith Xiques Villa, who came from Barranquilla on the Atlantic coast. His fans regretted his subsequent retirement from competition. In 2000, there was a bizarre incident in which he was kidnapped by FARC guerrillas. They held him for 24 hours, then released him unharmed.
He has subsequently become a businessman and hotelier, and a keen supporter of an initiative to develop young cyclists in his home department of Cundinamarca.

# 1985 Anno Mirabilis

But returning to Herrera and Parra, Colombia's international success continued in 1985. The first contest of the year between the Colombians and the Europeans started back home.

The Vuelta a Colombia was now an early season event, and a number of foreign teams joined the Vuelta that year, including a strong Spanish team, featuring Pedro "Perico" (the parakeet) Delgado. Delgado was a young rider on the way up. He had won the Vuelta a España only a few weeks before in a stunning comeback from six minutes down, and he was a climber (he would come second in the King of the Mountains in the Tour de France[7] a few weeks later). The Colombian team had also taken part in the Vuelta a España, and Fabio Parra had come 5th, while Herrera was forced to abandon due to tendonitis.

The Spaniards rode a disciplined race in the Vuelta a Colombia, and won 3 stages (two of them won by Vicente Belda of the second Spanish team, Kelme) but at the start of the 12th stage, ***there wasn't a single foreign rider in the top ten places.***

Herrera had taken the stage from Medellin to Riosucio over Minas. Coming into the penultimate day he was in 3rd place, a minute down from the leader. Fabio Parra was another 30 seconds behind him in 5th.

This stage was the Queen stage, the race over La Linea from west to east. Everybody felt they had a chance – or as Rafael Carrasco, the coach of the Kelme team put it, "the last chance."

There was no last chance for anyone except Herrera and Parra. They dropped the foreigners on the climb and went over the top of the Alto de Linea (3,100 metres) side by side.

The descent to Ibague is 63 kilometres long. Fabio Parra gave a master class in descending, and crossed the finish line a few seconds ahead of Herrera. Overall, Herrera was now the race leader, and Parra just 30 seconds behind.

The stage on the last day was the long climb from Ibague to Bogota. Again, Herrera and Parra finished almost together. It was heartbreak for Parra. Herrera had won the Vuelta by 33 seconds.

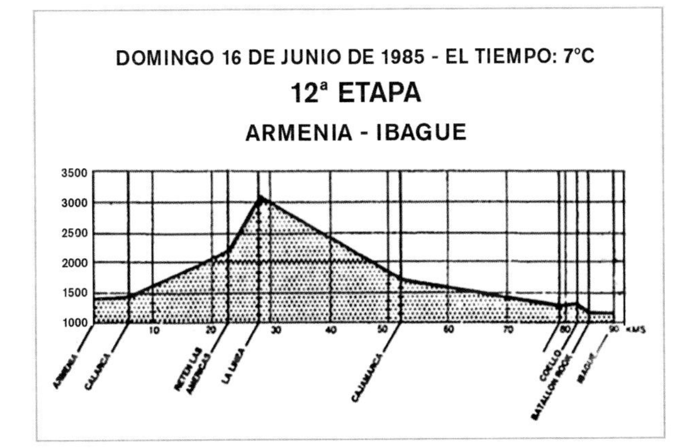


The Alto de la Linea from West to East is a hard climb from Manizales followed by a very long, fast descent. © *El Tiempo 16th June 1985*

Lucho Herrera in pain – date unknown
*Biblioteca Publica Piloto, Medellin*

7. Delgado went on to win the GC in the Tour de France in 1988 and the Vuelta a España for a second time in 1989.

Colombian cycling team in France, probably 1985. From the left: Fabio Parra (2nd), Patro Jiménez (4th), Alfonso Flórez (6th).
*Biblioteca Publica Piloto, Medellín*

GLORY DAYS

# Anno Mirabilis

The Tour de France took place four weeks later. Four time Tour winner Bernard Hinault was vying for his fifth win. Herrera and Parra were back in Europe, both competing for Team Colombia.

On the 11th stage, Herrera and Hinault worked together and Herrera won by 7 seconds. The next day, in a thrilling finish, the Colombians Parra and Herrera duelled up the final climb. Parra won the stage by a few seconds, and it was a Colombian 1-2. All of Colombia celebrated, and the celebrations continued the following day, when Herrera won a second stage, cementing his lead as King of the Mountains. Parra won the white jersey, "best young rider." Colombian cycling had finally shown the world what it could do.

Success breeds success. One of the two business conglomerates that dominate Colombian business came forward to sponsor what was effectively the national team. They called it Café de Colombia, one of their coffee brands. Not to be outdone, the other enterprise decided to sponsor a team as well. It was called Manzana Postobon, after its well-known pink drink brand.

Riding for Café de Colombia, Herrera and Parra blasted their way to new heights in international cycling in the next two years. Herrera won King of the Mountains and won the Vuelta a España in 1987, and went on to won KOM in the Tour de France.

In 1988, Herrera won the Vuelta a Colombia for the 4th time. It was a close run thing. The brilliant and youthful Alvaro Mejia had taken control of the race from halfway through, and looked set for his first victory at the age of 21. The stage on the penultimate day was a time trial which started in the main square of the tiny, beautiful colonial town of Villa de Leyva and ran 38 kilometres up the escarpment on the edge of the Cordillera Oriental, to Tunja. It was a cold afternoon, windy, with a persistent drizzle.

Coming into that stage, Herrera was 1 minute 31 seconds behind Mejia, a gap he had been unable to close over. But on that afternoon, Herrera showed his mastery. The road to Tunja winds up and up, onto the Altiplano, not far from the farmhouse where 18 months later the infant Nairo Quintana would be born. Herrera went over the top first and descended the last few kilometres into Tunja, 2 minutes and 45 seconds ahead of Mejia. The next day was his victory parade into Bogota.

Although Herrera was probably the best climber in the world at that time, he was not as consistent over the length of a Grand Tour as his countryman Fabio Parra. In 1988, Fabio Parra became the first Colombian to stand on the podium at the finish of the Tour de France in Paris. He was 3rd.

In 1989, he was subcampeon (2nd) in the Vuelta a España and finished in the top ten for the next 3 years.

Pascal Simon and Patrocinio Jiménez at the 1981 Tour de l'Avenir. Horacio Gil Ochoa wrote on the back: "Rivals and friends."
*Biblioteca Publica Piloto, Medellin*

Lucho Herrera's gig was mountains. He was King of the Mountains in the Giro d'Italia in 1989, and King of the Mountains in the Vuelta a España in 1991.

Lucho Herrera psyching up the opposition at the start.
*Biblioteca Publica Piloto, Medellin*

# 1990-1996 ISOLATION & DECLINE

## 1992 Superstars leave the stage while...

On 31st March 1992, Herrera and Parra lined up in Pereira for the opening stage of the Vuelta a Colombia.

It was 10 years since they had first ridden this race together. Herrera was riding for the Colombian team, Manzana Postobon, and Parra for a Spanish team.

The opening stage was an individual time trial, very short at 5.2 kilometres. Herrera won it in explosive style, taking the tricolour jersey. He held on to it for the next three stages, until he crashed and was forced to abandon.

Younger blood took over. But Parra, always canny, was biding his time. On the 11$^{th}$ stage, a longer time trial from Paipa to Tunja, he showed what he could do, winning the stage and the jersey.

He was still ahead as he cycled into Bogota the next day. It was his second and final victory in the Vuelta, a decade after his first. He and Herrera both retired that year. As well as their famous Grand Tour achievements, they had performed at the highest level in international cycling for 10 years.

One could say that Lucho Herrera came first more often – for example, in winning the Vuelta a Colombia four times, and the Vuelta a España once, in 1987. But in his other five Spanish appearances, his best placing was 12$^{th}$. Fabio Parra was more consistent. He had ridden in the Vuelta a España 8 times and came 2$^{nd}$ on one occasion and 5$^{th}$ on four others! But the pair of them were the leading lights of Colombian cycling and when they retired, you suddenly realised that it was dark outside.

During the 1990s, the Vuelta a Colombia lost popularity among the people of Colombia. Photos of today's stage winner no longer appeared on the front page of the papers or the headlines of the evening news.

It was the beginning of a long period of decline and isolation, not just for the Vuelta but for Colombian cycling in general.

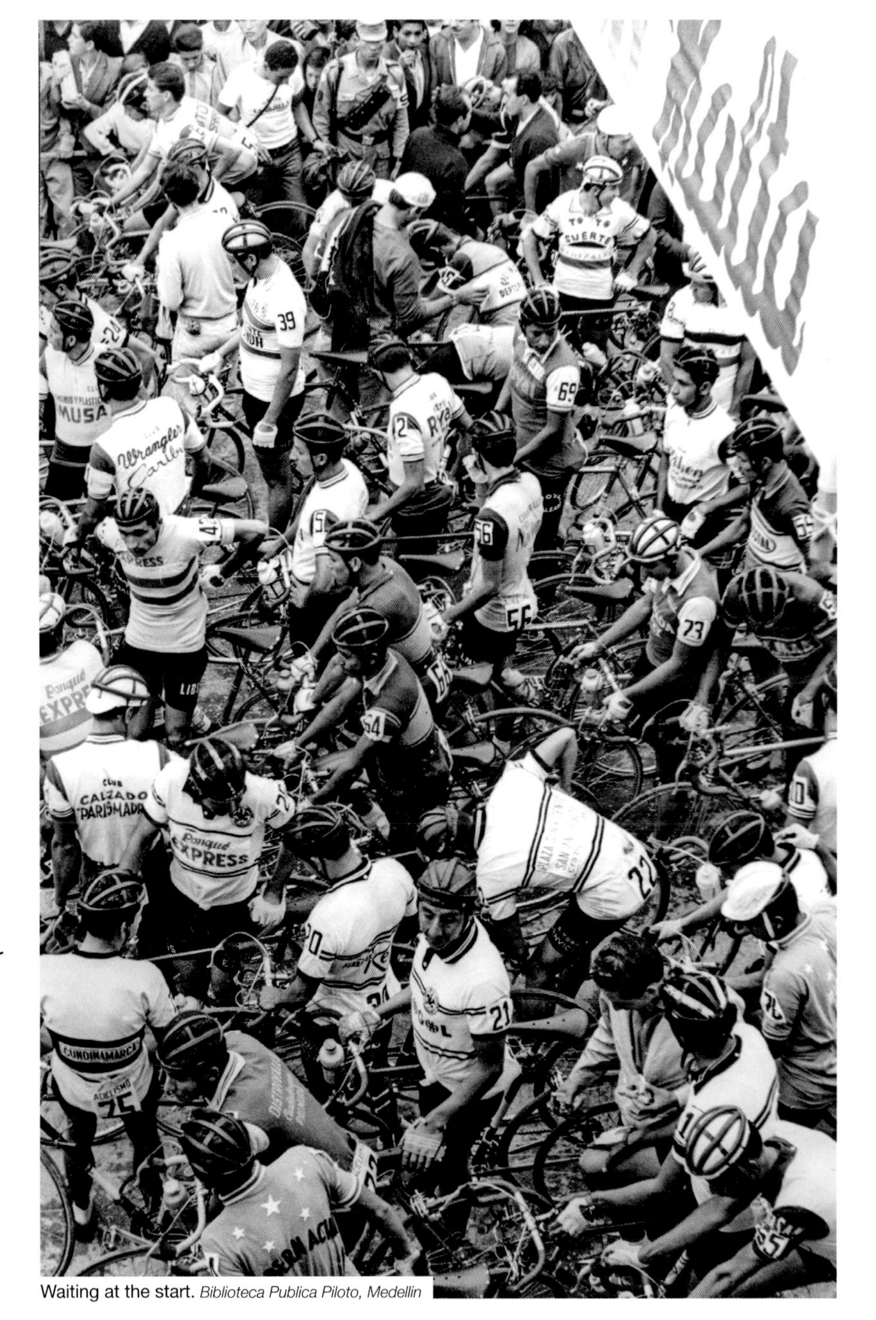

Waiting at the start. *Biblioteca Publica Piloto, Medellin*

# Those that live by the sword

At the end of the 1979 Vuelta, three of the **successful riders** (Armando Aristizábal, Gonzalo Marin and Alfonso Flórez) must have felt that the world was **at their feet**. Flórez had won the Vuelta. He and Marin both won stages, and Aristizábal was runner up in the sprints competition.

**Armando Aristizábal** soon gave up competitive cycling and got a job as **team director** of Punto Sports Catalina, a **cycling team** owned by a **drug dealer**, Hugo Hernán Valencia. During a race near Medellin, Valencia, his bodyguard, Armando Aristizábal and a cameraman were **kidnapped**.

The **bodyguard** was **killed immediately**, but it was three weeks before the **bodies** of the other three were found on a **rubbish heap** in Poblado, a nearby suburb of Medellin. They had been **tortured**. Pablo Escobar's chief hitman, "Popeye", later confirmed that Escobar's organisation had carried out the killing.

**Gonzalo Marín** – who had ridden for Roberto Escobar's Ositto team – was rumoured to have got a **job** with the **Medellin cartel**. He was **gunned down** on April 25, 1990, apparently by his employers in a dispute over missing cash.

**Alfonso Flórez** was **shot** in 1992 inside his wife's car. He was said to have made love to the **wrong woman** and her **gangster** husband **disapproved**.

And these were just three of the casualties that tarnished the reputation of Colombian cycling and **frightened foreign riders** and indeed sponsors.

**Ricardo Zea**, who had succeeded Julio Arrastia as the Antioquian coach and who had trained Ramón Hoyos, became in later years the **manager** of the Escobars' stables and farms. He was **assassinated**, probably by Los Pepes, the vigilante group which murdered many of Pablo's associates.

In 1991, the Manzana **Postobon team** was **arrested** on its way to the Vuelta a Murcia, in **Spain.** One suitcase – that of 29 year old Juan Carlos Castillo – was found to contain **several kilos of cocaine**.

**Juan Carlos Castillo** had been a **domestique** for **Herrera** during the golden years of the 1980s. Castillo spent 4 months in gaol but was eventually **acquitted** and went to live in Pereira. He was **shot dead** by an unknown **assassin** in 1993.

On October 24, 1991, a team of **10 Colombian cyclists**, was detained at **Rome** airport. Their **bikes** were found to be **stuffed with cocaine**. Small beer, perhaps, compared to **Carlos Julio Siachoque**. Siachoque had ridden for Droguería Yaneth in the late '70s. In 1996, **police found a ton** of high quality **cocaine** in his apartment. He was sentenced to **9 years in gaol.**

# 1992 ...drug wars destroy the theatre...

**Reasons are easy to find.**

For a start, there was the mayhem surrounding the demise of the Medellin cartel. It started with the attacks by Pablo Escobar on the government and the security services, and concluded with the counter-attack by the Los Pepes vigilantes (whoever they were).

Drug related violence in Colombia was so common that it made only domestic headlines. But in 1989 the mid-air destruction of Avianca Flight 203 hit the international press. So did the massive truck bomb which exploded outside the security services HQ in Bogota a month later. It killed 52 people and injured 1,000. These disasters made headlines around the world.

Not surprisingly, foreign teams stayed away. Compare 1996, say, with 1986. In '86, there were 20 teams in the Vuelta, of which 10 were professional, and five were European. In '96, there were 15 teams, but they were all Colombian, all amateur, and no European riders at all.

The violence affected some Colombian cyclists more personally. Sponsorship by the drug lords had brought the riders themselves into friendly contact with the traffickers. Professional cycling was dangerous and the rewards were small. Drug running was also dangerous, but the cartels were awash with cash. As their professional careers waned, some riders found themselves tempted into a violent world whose rules they did not understand until too late.

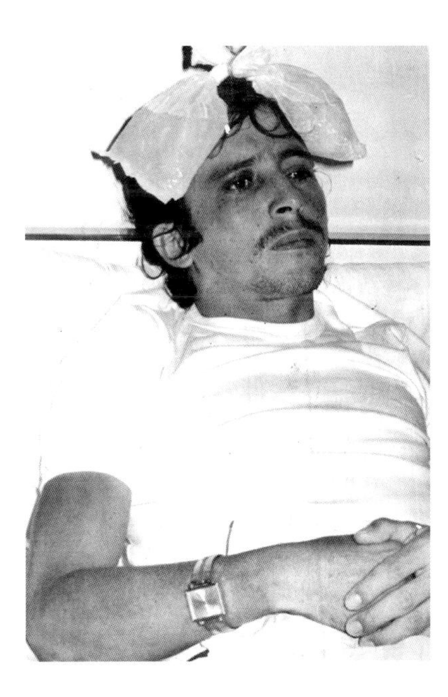

Gonzalo Marin was a brilliant cyclist who got too close to the narco traffickers. Seen here in 1975, during his cycling heyday.
*Photo José Betancur*

En política lo importante no es tener razón sino que se la den a uno
KONRAD ADENAUER

EL TIEMPO

CARRUSEL

78 PAGINAS - 6 SECCIONES

VIERNES 13 DE MARZO DE 1987

$ 60.00

**Gobierno bajó el reintegro cafetero**

Nueva política de comercialización

Por JOSE SUAREZ
Redactor de EL TIEMPO

Colombia bajó ayer en 25 centavos de dólar el precio mínimo de exportación de su café y anunció la adopción de una nueva política de comercialización en ese campo, orientada a flexibilizar y facilitar el manejo de la situación cafetera a los vaivenes del mercado mundial de este producto.

El nuevo reintegro cafetero quedó en 1.10 dólares la libra, precio muy parecido a la cotización externa que se viene registrando en los últimos días. Antes estaba en 1.35 dólares por libra.

Al hacer el anuncio, el ministro de Hacienda, César Gaviria Trujillo, dijo que el país ha comenzado a colocarse a tono con lo que sucede en el mercado mundial del café y anticipó que vendrán otras medidas para flexibilizar la comercialización del grano.

Una de estas medidas será la de permitir variar el reintegro casi que automáticamente con las oscilaciones del precio internacional, para permitir así que el país esté permanentemente en el mercado.

La medida del reintegro fue la única que se comunicó ayer. Posteriormente vendrán otras, entre estas la variación de la retención cafetera. Más tarde se entrará a considerar variables de política interna, tales como el precio de sustentación y el mantenimiento o desmonte de los Títulos de Ahorro Cafetero, TAC.

Los exportadores privados consideraron de inmediato que la simple reducción del reintegro no es suficiente, y que se requiere modificaciones en la retención, especialmente en la parte de esta que se paga en dinero y que se denomina como "la cuchilla".

El gerente de Fedecafé, Jorge Cárdenas Gutiérrez, dijo por su parte que el país se colocó en condiciones de competencia. Del TAC, el precio interno y la retención, manifestó que no se habían tratado. (Página 8-A)

**Oleada terrorista en Bogotá**

*Bomberos apagan las llamas que ayer destruyeron uno de los dos buses de servicio TSS interceptados en las instalaciones de la Universidad Nacional, en la capital de la república, por guerrilleros que el martes pasado también dinamitaron dos alcaldías menores y una subestación de Policía en la víspera de la conmemoración de la muerte del jefe del M-19 Alvaro Fayad Delgado. En los atentados, que no tuvieron ninguna vinculación con las labores académicas del Alma Mater, no hubo heridos ni detenidos.*

***Secuestran 4 miembros de un equipo de ciclismo en Medellín: un muerto***

MEDELLIN, 12 (Por Gustavo Ramírez O.).— Dos directivos, un conductor y un camarógrafo del equipo de ciclismo de la empresa Punto Sport Catalina, de Cali, que llegaron a reintegrarse a la IV Clásica de Itagüí, fueron secuestrados hoy por un presunto comando guerrillero del Ejército de Liberación Nacional (ELN), al sur de esta capital, y uno de ellos, horas después fue hallado asesinado, informó la Policía.

John Jairo Cartagena Maya, 34, fue acribillado de 30 tiros en Itagüí, a pocos kilómetros del lugar en que fue secuestrado.

Según el inspector de Policía, Ramón Agudelo, Cartagena Maya, un conductor, fue tirado a un basurero del barrio Santa Cruz.

Los victimarios arrojaron el cadáver al parecer desde un vehículo y se ignora cuales fueron las causas para que lo mataran en la forma que tradicionalmente ejecutan a sus víctimas las bandas locales del narcotráfico.

Hugo Hernando Valencia, ejecutivo y accionista mayoritario de Punto Sport Catalina, el administrador del equipo, el exciclista profesional Armando Aristizabal, el camarógrafo Jorge Figueroa, y Cartagena Maya cayeron en poder de siete hombres cuando se preparaban para la segunda jornada de la clásica de ciclismo.

La Policía Metropolitana dijo que los delincuentes se identificaron como miembros del ELN, eran jóvenes y amenazaron a sus víctimas con revólveres y metralletas. Página 8-A

*Los sin tocayo...*

**Preside el Celam**

*Monseñor Darío Castrillón Hoyos, obispo de Pereira, fue nombrado ayer presidente del Consejo Episcopal Latinoamericano, Celam, para un período de cuatro años, durante la XXI asamblea de los cardenales y obispos del Continente que se realiza en Asunción, Paraguay.* Página 8-A

**Estafan a Volkswagen en US$ 260 millones**

BRAUNSCHWEIG, RFA, 12 (AFP).— Para hacer frente a una de las estafas más cuantiosas y espectaculares de los últimos tiempos en la República Federal Alemana, la firma Volkswagen constituyó un fondo de 480 millones de marcos (260 millones de dolares) para enjugar su pérdida cambiaria, se informó hoy aquí.

La reserva equivale al 80 por ciento del beneficio neto consolidado de 1985, anunció lacónicamente la dirección, mostrándose luego especialmente parca en informaciones.

Para el cuarto grupo automovilístico mundial, que pierde en un solo golpe, además de la enorme masa de dinero, la imagen de excelente administrador, lo esencial consiste ahora en limitar lo más posible los daños, en momentos en que el curso de sus acciones baja espectacularmente.

Ayer, después de la revelación de la estafa, la acción de Volkswagen perdió más del 7 por ciento de su valor en una sola sesión.

Por su parte la justicia alemana tendrá una tarea ciclópea por (Página 9-C)

**En páginas interiores**

- Cayó parte del estatuto sobre armas (Página 2-A)
- Name vs Slebi, una rivalidad de años... (Página 8-A)
- Lusinchi destaca relaciones con Colombia (Ultima-C)
- Cadena 3 de TV no será ampliada (Página 9-C)

***En Urabá: el Estado es privado***

Por LUCIA VICTORIA TORRES
(Enviada especial)

APARTADO, Antioquia. — Aquí es difícil hacerse a la idea ... año entrega más de US$ 220 millones al país por cultivar una fruta que da la cara por él en el exterior

*"Four members of a cycle team kidnapped in Medellín, one is dead".*

Turbulent Times: El Tiempo on 13th March 1987. The export price of coffee is cut, a bus in Bogota is destroyed by a bomb and a cycling team in Medellin is kidnapped. The team bodyguard, says the article, was found dead with 30 bullets in his body.
*Casa Editorial El Tiempo S.A.*

# José-Jaime González Pico

## Born
28th July, 1968
Sogamosa, Boyacá
2,480 metres.

## Nickname
Chepe.

## Vuelta a Colombia wins
1994, 1995 and he was King of the Mountains in 1992, 1993 and 1994.

## Early days
One of Chepe's boyhood idols was Fabio Parra, who was also from Sogamosa, and he dreamed of racing himself. His uncle Epimenio González, who had been a pro cyclist, encouraged him and he started riding, aged 13. His first sponsor was the owner of the local laundry. After some successes in local races, he won a place with the Lotería de Boyacá team and did well.

## Career
Chepe turned professional in 1992 and rode for 2 years for Manzana Postobon, until their dissolution. He raced in Europe as well as domestically. In 1995 he joined the Spanish/Colombian Kelme team and was spectacularly successful, winning the Vuelta a Colombia in 1994 and 1995. Both years he was also King of the Mountains and won 5 stages in total. In 1996, he rode in the Giro d'Italia, Tour Suissa and finished 15th in the World Championship road race. He continued European success with Kelme, being King of the Mountains in the Giro twice and runner up twice. He won a stage of the Tour de France in 1996 thanks to quick thinking – he overheard the team car of the Spanish champion giving instructions in Spanish for a surprise attack and followed them himself!

## Vuelta a Colombia stages
7 stage wins, beginning in 1990.

## Grand Tour wins
Stage 11 (Tour de France 1996)
Stage 20 & KOM (Giro 1997)
Stage 5 & KOM (Giro 1998)

## Later days
When he retired as a professional cyclist, he got a job as the Team Director for the Colombian Armed Forces cycling team.

# ...bringing death and isolation

So drugs and drug related violence were one reason for the massive decline of Colombian cycling in the 1990s. Another was cash or rather the absence of it.

Two competing national conglomerates has funded Colombia's immensely successful European teams (Café de Colombia and Manzana Postobon) during the 1980s. Having the two of them in competition created a virtuous circle: more money, better results, more money. When the sponsor of Café de Colombia withdrew funding in 1990, the circle was broken. Manzana Postobon continued abroad for two more years but after the Rome airport smuggling scandal (see above) and gaol sentence of Juan Carlos Castillo, their sponsor also called a halt.

So from 1993 onwards, there were no Colombian national teams competing in Europe. And back home in Colombia, most of the narco-traffickers were all dead or in gaol. So the magic money tree that was Parfumeria Yaneth, Bicicletas Ositto and the like dried up also.

There was also more competition from other sports. The Vuelta a Colombia and its upstart sister race, the Clásico RCN, had captivated the nation.
The sheer adulation, the hysteria that greeted el Zipa, Ramón Hoyos, el Niño and Cochise gave every cycle messenger or farm boy with a bike something to dream about. But soccer had gradually been gaining ground and slowly the nation's airwaves became more dedicated to the ball than the bike.

The combination of these factors impoverished these great domestic events. Now they were run on a shoestring, and the foreigners and the crowds stayed at home.

But a Colombian rider could still compete in Europe and be famous, by signing up with a foreign team. If they had the talent. Oliverio Rincon and Alvaro Mejia had the talent. Rincon won the Vuelta in 1989, aged 21. Alvaro Mejia won the 1988 and 1989 Clásico RCN.

Rincon and Mejia were hired by foreign teams, who set their priorities. They were – until proven champions – domestiques. Their job was to support the team effort, to shelter, supply and lead out the team's no 1 star.

They worked hard abroad, riding for foreign teams but somehow never reached the podium of the Grand Tours (although Rincon won stages in all three). Nor did they come back, year after year, to set the country alight with their prowess over Letras or the Alto de Minas, leaving the Europeans gasping for air behind them.

"Alfonso Flórez was assassinated yesterday"

2B/EL TIEMPO/VIERNES 24 DE ABRIL DE 1992

DEPORTES

EXTRA
Tiempo

▶ **SI IRA A LOS OLIMPICOS** el técnico Jorge García Beltrán, quien dirigió a los boxeadores de Colombia que estuvieron en el preolímpico de Mendoza (Argentina), según declaraciones a *RCN* de Mario Flórez, presidente de la Federación Colombiana de Boxeo. Flórez agregó que sería nombrado como asistente técnico el cubano Adrián Ponce, quien trbaja con la Liga de Bogotá.

▶ **APLAZARON LA ELIMINATORIA** mundial supermosca del Consejo Mundial de Boxeo (CMB) entre el mexicano José Luis Bueno y el colombiano Elvis Alvarez. El combate pasó del 4 al 11 de mayo. En la función actuará otro criollo, el mosca Jesús Zúniga.

▶ **EL AJEDRECISTA** Gildardo García fue acreditado por la Federación Colombiana de este deporte ante la FIDE como Gran Maestro. El año anterior García tenía un elo de 2.485 puntos. Pero en la Copa Latinoamericana, celebrada en Bogotá a mediados de diciembre, perdió 10 puntos. Sin embargo, en el 'Duelo de Reyes', contra Alonso Zapatza, ganó 7,4. Además, en el Abierto de Palma de Mayorca Español, donde fue campeón, García obtuvo 22,2, para un total de 2.505 puntos.

**Por sicarios en Medellín**

## Asesinado ayer Alfonso Flórez

*El ex ciclista recibió cuatro balazos en la cabeza y murió instantáneamente. No hay pistas de los asesinos.*

Medellín

En hechos que al cierre de la presente edición aún no eran muy claros para las autoridades, fue asesinado ayer en esta ciudad, poco después de las 7 de la noche, el ex pedalista santandereano Alfonso Flórez Ortiz.

Flórez, bicampeón de la Vuelta a Colombia y vencedor de la Vuelta al Porvenir en Francia en 1980, fue baleado por sicarios en el cruce de la carrera 65 con las calles 48 y 47D, en cercanías de la Villa Olímpica.

Los hechos del asesinato del deportista eran muy confusos. El ex ciclista quedó en el interior de su vehículo, un Mazda color blanco de modelo reciente identificado con placas QAD-902. Recibió cuatro impactos de bala en la cabeza, que le produjeron la muerte en forma instantánea.

Dos sicarios que se movilizaban en una moto lo abordaron por la parte izquierda del vehículo, le dispararon repetidamente y emprendieron la huida.

Pese a que inmediatamente después del hecho las autoridades de la capital antioqueña desplegaron un vasto operativo para dar captura a los asesinos, las pesquisas fueron infructuosas.

Flórez se retiró de la actividad en 1987 y desde entonces se dedicó a los negocios particulares en Medellín, donde residía. Estaba casado con Martha Tarazona y tenía dos hijas. Había nacido el 5 de noviembre de 1952.

Archivo / EL TIEMPO

**FUE EL PRIMER COLOMBIANO** en subir a los más alto del podio en una prueba por etapas en Europa. El 21 de septiembre de 1980, Alfonso Flórez ganó el Tour del Avenir.

**Reacciones de sus amigos y allegados**

## 'Era un hombre recto': Cárdenas

Con gran sorpresa y conmoción se conoció anoche sobre las 7:30 la noticia del asesinato del ex ciclista Alfonso Flórez Ortiz.

Porque el doble campeón de la Vuelta a Colombia (79 y 83) y el primer ganador por este país del Tour de L'Avenir (80), "era de una rectitud impresionante", según dijo anoche Elkin Darío Rendón, uno de los más cercanos amigos del Flórez.

Y en verdad causó consternación en todo el país. Todo agravado por el paro de teléfonos, que dificultó la averiguación de los hechos y la comunicación entre los familiares de Flórez, quienes desde Bucaramanga hicie- Manzana Postobón Aficionado, dijo en declaraciones dadas a *RCN*: "Lamentable lo que le pasó a Alfonso porque él era de una rectitud impresionante, pero esto es causa de la inseguridad de Medellín. El miércoles hablamos por teléfono y charlamos de deportes. La verdad es que no nos explicamos que pudo haber pasado con él.

"Desde que dejó de corrrer no quiso volver al ciclismo. El se venía mucho a mi casa, incluso a mi señora le decía 'mamá'. La verdad es que Alfonso simplemente se mantenía alejado de las competencias", agregó Rendón.

## Flórez, otro eslabón de la trágica cadena

Otros siete ex pedalistas colombianos han sido asesinados desde 1985, pero ninguno alcanzó el renombre y la fama del santandereano Alfonso Flórez Ortiz, quien cayó muerto anoche en una calle de Medellín víctima de los sicarios.

El primero de esta triste lista fue Faustino Cristancho, campeón de la Vuelta de la Juventud de 1973. El ex pedalista fue baleado en Bogotá por desconocidos el 22 de mayo de 1985.

Año y medio después de ese suceso, exactamente el 21 de septiembre de 1986, la víctima fue el joven Víctor Julio Hernández, vinculado por ese entonces al equipo aficionado de Pilas Varta, uno de los pioneros del pedalismo profesional en el país. El asesinato ocurrió en Medellín.

Uno de los casos más sonados de asesinatos de deportistas en Colombia se produjo el 7 de abril de 1987. Ese día fueron encontrado en El Poblado (Medellín), los cadáveres del ex ciclista y técnico Armando Aristizábal y el camarógrafo Jorge Enrique Figueroa. Ellos dos habían sido secuestrados días antes en compañía del dirigiente Hugo Hernán Valencia durante una de las etapas de la Clásica de Itagüí.

La trágica cadena de asesinatos de deportistas continuó en 1989, cuando Aureliano Gallón, un pedalista de la época del gran Ramón Hoyos Vallejo, es decir, la década de los 50, fue ultimado a balazos en Cali.

Y en los más recientes hechos de esa naturaleza, dos ilustres figuras del lote nacional, Gonzalo Marín y Manuel Ignacio 'El Sardino' Gutiérrez, también cayeron muertos en confusos episodios que nunca fueron aclarados por las autoridades.

Ahora, sin razones aparentes, el que se conocía en el medio ciclístico como un hombre bueno que no le hacía mal a nadie, Alfonso Flórez Ortiz, fue baleado ayer en Medellín, su patria chica por adopción.

El Tiempo 24 April 1992. The report on the murder of Alfonso Flórez lists 6 other professional cyclists killed since 1985.
*Casa Editorial El Tiempo S.A.*

AROUND COLOMBIA

# Boyacá, gems and history

The Andean department of Boyacá lies on the cordillera Oriental, just to the north of Bogota. In the west, it is high (2,800 metres) upland country with rolling hills. A jagged extension stretches out – and down – to the hothouse of the Magdalena River. To the east, the vast Llanos (plains) spread out to the border with neighbouring Casanare, and beyond.

Home of champions: the rolling hills and farms of Boyacá.
*Photo Biblioteca Publica Piloto, Medellin*

Charming Villa de Leyva, a tiny town with a big square.
*Photo Cyclota.com*

Boyacá was the site of some famous battles during Colombia's War of Independence and in particular the battle of the "Puente de Boyacá," (the bridge of Boyacá,) where Simon Bolivar and General Santander defeated the Spanish in 1819, and entered Bogota in triumph 3 days later. It was the beginning of Gran Colombia, the supersized independent republic envisioned by Bolivar.

Boyacá has a collection of beautiful little colonial towns, like the Villa de Leyva and Monguí – and the capital, Tunja, which is a treasure trove of richly decorated churches and houses.

Boyacá is famous for its emeralds. Boyacá mines more emeralds than anywhere else on earth. The emerald mines are down around Muzo, in the western corner.

In the north-east corner of Boyacá lies the El Cocuy national park. This mountainous Andean wilderness is hard core. You go in, you sign the book. If you don't come back after a few days, they send out men on mules to look for you. If you are lucky.

### *Cycling notes*

*Boyacá also contains Sogamosa, the cycling capital of Colombia, and nearby the patron saint of cyclists, the Virgin of Morca. Many of Colombia's most famous cyclists came from the highlands of Boyacá, including Miguel Samacá, José Patrocinio Jiménez, Fabio Parra and more recently Nairo Quintana.*

The farmhouse above Combita, Boyacá where Nairo Quintana was brought up. *Photo Stephen Norman*

1994-1995

# Champion Chepe

Somewhat of an exception to this gloomy pattern was José Jaime (Chepe) González. Chepe was a child of Sogamoso, a cycling town in Boyacá. In 1995 he left Manzana Postobon and joined Kelme, a Spanish team which a decade later was to sink in a swamp of doping allegations (see the next chapter). A superb climber, Chepe won King of the Mountains in the Giro d'Italia, and won stages in the Tour de France and the Giro. And he did come home to win the Vuelta a Colombia in 1994 and again in 1995, albeit in a field devoid of European competition.

Perhaps the appetite of the Colombian public had been spoiled by the rich diet of Herrera and Parra. Everyone likes a winner. Colombian cyclists in the 1990s were not winning Grand Tours, and there were no foreigners coming to be humiliated domestically, and so the public turned off.

*But there was another, more sinister force at work.*

Chepe Gonzalez riding for Manzana Postobon c. 1993. *Photo Alberto Urrego.*

Henry Cardenas (nickname 'Cebollita' or Little Onion) retired from European cycling in the 1990s because he knew he couldn't win clean… *Mundo Ciclistico*

# 1996 The Europeans had become supermen...

Henry Cardenas was a successful Colombian cyclist who rode with Herrera and Café de Colombia in Europe during the '80s. In 2006, he gave a dramatic account[8] of the effects of EPO doping on European racing:

*All of a sudden, many patacones [which literally means fried plantains], as we used to call the faceless riders who were pack filler, started leaving us behind in the mountains.*
*On the flat, the speeds became astonishing. In one stage that was completely flat, without as much as an overpass or bridge, my speedometer read 50 miles an hour (80 kilometres an hour). I simply couldn't believe it, so I went to a teammate and asked to look at his speedometer. They all showed the same, we really were going at 50 miles an hour.*

Particularly galling to a Colombian were the climbs:

*...it seemed like everyone, just everyone, could beat us. They could all climb faster. I remember in one race...I found myself in great difficulty in a climb early on. Dimitri Konyshev, who was a sprinter, told one Italian rider: "Look at this Colombian, just a couple of years ago he would have humiliated us in the mountains, and now he can barely keep up with us!" ...I replied "I prefer being dead last clean, than win and later find myself in a hospital bed!" Konyshev told me I was right, and that cycling was rotten to the core.*

Cardenas had harsh words for the Colombian press:

*...even more maddening was the way I was criticized by the press, at least certain Colombian journalists, who were not capable of understanding the fundamental change that was happening in cycling, I'm speaking of the new types of doping that became popular in the 1990s. They didn't have the guts to explain Colombian fans why our riders could no longer ride and compete like in the days of Lucho and Fabio Parra. They accused us of being lazy, and of having become bourgeois over time. It was incredibly unfair.*

He linked their inability to win with the collapse of national sponsorship:

*Sadly, it was then that they ended the Cafe De Colombia and the Postobon team. That was because we Colombians insisted in winning, and the fans did too, so the teams ended. We couldn't win. We'd won the Dauphine, the Vuelta, stages in grand tours... and suddenly we were coming in 30th. People don't like that. That's no good to a sponsor. But people didn't realize that the speeds in the peloton had become absolutely inhuman. On the flats it was insane, on the big climbs it could be 25 miles an hour (40 kilometres an hour) or even more. It was impossible to even stay on their wheel.*

And the public had become contemptuous:

*All of a sudden, we were being treated very badly, even out in the street when we went out training. I remember little boys, almost babies who were barely old enough to speak, yelling all kinds of things to us in the street, cursing at us. It was impossible to argue, or even talk to people in those days. During the race we did here in Colombia, everyone was insulting us. They threw beer at us, and heckled us as we went by. We were hated.*

Cardenas decided he had to get out of Europe:

*Eventually, I chose to retire. I didn't touch a bicycle for a full year, from the extreme disappointment that I felt. I was offered deals with other teams in Europe, but I knew what that would mean. I would have to inject the same things as everyone else on those teams. I didn't touch my bike at all in 1993. In 1994, I came back to racing, but only in Colombia.*

8. Conducted by Altimetrias de Colombia and later translated into English and republished by Alps & Andes, reproduced here with their permission.

# A brief guide to doping

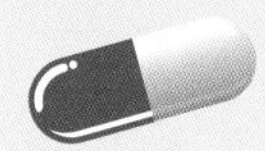

**The array of performance enhancing drugs is bewildering to the average reader. Here are some of the drugs which have appeared during this period:**

**Testosterone.** Goes back a long way. Builds muscle strength and enhances aerobic performance.

**EPO. Erythropoietin.** EPO is a natural hormone produced in the kidneys that stimulates production of red blood cells in the bone marrow. More red blood cells (=increased hematocrit score) means more oxygen carrying capacity.

**Microdosing (EPO).** To avoid detection, an athlete may inject small doses each day.

**Blood transfusions.** Another way of boosting red blood cells. Blood is removed from the athlete and stored – cold – for up to a month. The body produces new red blood cells to compensate. Then the stored blood is re-introduced and the athlete has more oxygen carrying capacity – temporarily. As the authorities wised up to EPO and blood transfusions, doping has evolved. AICAR, GW501516 (also known as Endurobol) and CERA have entered the fray.

**AICAR** stimulates mitochondria, the component of muscular cells responsible for aerobic energy production.

**HES (hydroxyethyl starch)** an anticoagulant substitute for blood plasma which can mask the taking of EPO by reducing the haematocrit score.

**GW501516 (Cardarine)** is different. It encourages the body to burn fat for energy, and so enables athletes to train harder and increase muscle mass. But it has also been shown to create tumours in lab tests.

**Ephedrine.** A chemical extract from the ma huang herb. It's a stimulant said to produce improved aerobic performance and reduce fatigue. Not dissimilar to caffeine.

**The Colombian public and press may not have been ecstatic about domestic racing during this period, but there were some thrilling races and a lot of doping.**

# 1997-2016 WHOSE TURN IS IT ANYWAY?

## 1997 The Kelme boys come home...

Henry Cardenas quit cycling in Europe because he couldn't win – not without doping[9]. Other riders who had raced in Europe decided not to retire. Instead they moved back to Colombia.

The first big winner was José -Jaime "Chepe" Gonzalez, a Colombian rider who caught the tail end of the European wave. As already mentioned, Chepe won the Vuelta a Colombia in 1995 and again in 1996.

He was not alone. Riding with him in Kelme[10] in 1995 were Hernán Buenahora, Libardo Niño and José Castelblanco. The Kelme team went through various iterations and sponsorship changes. In 1998, it was Kelme-Costa Blanca. Chepe was still riding for it, and so were Oscar Sevilla and Santiago Botero, two more future winners of the Vuelta a Colombia.

This group of six riders was to dominate the Vuelta a Colombia from 1997 to 2015. José Castelblanco, who hailed from the uplands of Boyacá, was the most successful, winning four times, followed by the triple victories of his friend Hernán Buenahora (also from Boyacá), and the Spaniard Oscar Sevilla. Felix Cardenas won the trophy twice.

They were all seniors. Castelblanco was 27 when he won the Vuelta in 1997 and 36 at the time of his 4th and final victory. Four of them would have won more often or earlier, but tested positive for some banned substance or other.

### Bad habits learned abroad

The records of Colombian road racing from 1998 until 2015 shows that doping was not tackled with the same vigour as it (eventually) was in Europe.

The problem with doping is that it works. So an ambitious athlete is posed with a stark choice: shall I dope and have a chance of winning? Or not, and gamble that no-one else is? Critical to stamping out doping is a rigorous program of testing which reassures the athlete that they are better off clean because (a) they are likely to get caught and (b) the rest of the peleton has made the same calculation. It's a group thing.

If everyone else is doing it, you would be (logically) foolish not to. If no-one else is (and the controls are tight and the penalties large) you would foolish to try. The cycling authorities in Colombia are not wealthy. And during this period, they were quite isolated. For 20 years, they struggled to create a clean culture. Sometimes they were not trying very hard.

In 2013, Ramiro Valencia, newly appointed President of the Colombian Cycling Federation, addressed a dinner at which young cyclists from the Coldeportes Claro team were present:

*"It is neither mine nor the Federation's objective to control doping and drugs. Absolutely not. Why? Because I cannot conceive a sport that is drugged. I think it is more important to focus on the sportsman as an individual and help him throughout his career to become a better person"*

*"...Sport is a means of achieving better citizens. That is our objective.... And that goes far beyond drug control. That we must implement of course and make sure it happens."*

*"Coldeportes must be responsible for that, not us...Doping is at the lowest level of the sport and therefore not my responsibility."*

Claro team dinner, Tour de Juventidad, 2013
Ramiro Valencia, then President of the Colombian Cycling Federation explains why doping is not his responsibility. Cochise to his right doesn't look impressed! *Youtube*

9. Henry Cardenas went back to Colombia and had some success with the Gaseosas Glacias team. He won the Vuelta a Tolima, and was subcampeon in the Clásico RCN in 1995.

10. The Kelme team achieved notoriety in 2004 when one of its riders, Jesus Manzano, blew the whistle on it, exposing a culture of systemic doping. Although disbelieved at first, his revelations led to the investigation by Spanish police known as Operacion Puerto. The police seized 100+ blood bags, neatly labelled, plus EPO, steroids and human growth hormones in Dr Fuentes' Madrid clinic. Dr Fuentes was the team doctor of the Kelme cycling team. It is said that 58 cyclists were clients of Dr Fuentes, along with tennis players, footballers and other sportsmen. However the Spanish courts ultimately absolved Fuentes on the grounds that his activities were not a crime under Spanish law. The judge in charge of the case ordered the evidence destroyed.

11. The Colombian government department responsible for the development of sport in the country.

## José Joaquin Castelblanco Romero

### Born
15 Dec 1969
Umbita, Boyacá
2,480 metres

### Nickname
Don José

### Vuelta a Colombia podium 4

### Grand Tour wins
None. His best results: Tour de France (27th), Giro d'Italia (15th) and Vuelta (14th)

### Early days
José Castelblanco was born into a farming family, the second of 8 children. As a child, he wanted to be a farmer but when he was 11, he left for Bogota, with his parents' consent, saying he was bored of growing potatoes, sugarcane and peas. Life was hard. He stayed with friends, got a job in a bakery and became a baker. Then later he got a job as a messenger boy for a pharmacy. With a loan, he bought his first touring bike and started racing. He won the Doble a Duitama and that got him enough recognition to get signed by Pony Malta.

### Vuelta a Colombia stages: 8

### Career
One of Colombia's most prolific and consistent cyclists, he competed for 25 years. With Pony Malta, he won the Vuelta a Guatemala (1992) and the Vuelta a Guadeloupe (1994). In 1995, he won a place on the Spanish professional team, Kelme, although he was dropped by them in Dec 1996. He joined a Colombian team, Telecom-Flavia, and in 1997 he was Colombian Road Racing champion and won his first Vuelta a Colombia. In 1999 he won the Vuelta a Colombia again, and rejoined Kelme. He rode in numerous Grand Tours, primarily with Kelme, including completing the Giro d'Italia 4 times.
During the 2010s, he repeatedly attempted to win the Vuelta a Colombia again, in the company of his friend Hernán Buenahora and rival Libardo Niño. He succeeded in 2002, and again in 2004, only to be disqualified by a positive test for testosterone. In 2006 he finally succeeded (4th GC win). He kept trying after that. He was 4th in 2007 when Santiago Botero won for the first time.

### Later days
After 25 years of cycling, Don José retired in 2008, after a fall in which he broke his collarbone and had surgery 3 times in 6 months. He went on to coach a youth team in Colombia.

# Round and round we go

Ramiro Valencia resigned in 2015.

## 1997. Castelblanco

Riding for Kelme, Castelblanco dominated the 1997 Vuelta, leading the race for 13 stages.

## 1998. Castelblanco

Another decisive victory for Don José, this time by 8 minutes.

## 2000. Palacio

Hector Iván Palacio the Plane[12] won the millennium Vuelta by 2 seconds, the tightest win in the history of the race up to that date (but read on!). His team, 05 Orbitel, took the first 4 places in the GC. It was Palacio's tenth attempt! He had been 2nd in 96 and 3rd in 97.

## 2001. Buenahora

*Poche parole, molti fatti.* Few words, many deeds. The Italian coach of Hernán Buenahora used these words to describe his pupil's achievement in winning the 2001 Vuelta a Colombia at the comparatively mature age of 34. He dominated the 2001 Vuelta, taking the tricolour jersey halfway through and holding it to the end. He won four stages, including the final time trial from Bogota to the Alto de los Patios, a popular 400 metre climb out of the city.

Buenahora had had a distinguished career. Back in 1990, he was riding for Café de Colombia and had won a stage in the Vuelta a Colombia that year and come 3rd in the King of the Mountains. He served as a domestique in Europe during the 1990s, competing six times in the Tour de France and the Giro d'Italia, and five times in the Vuelta a España.

Buenahora's team was sponsored by Selle Italia, an Italian saddle manufacture.
He remained competitive in the Vuelta for a long time, winning stages in 2005, 2007 and 2008.

## 2002. Castelblanco

But the next year, 2002, Castelblanco was back in dominant form, also riding for Selle Italia. He blasted the opposition in the two time trials, winning the 17.5 kilometre time trial from Cali to "Kilometre 18" by 49 seconds. He wore the leader's jersey for 8 stages in total, including the final climb up another of Colombia's ramps, the ascent of the Loma del Escobero[13]. His winning margin was an impressive 4 minutes and 13 seconds.

José Castelblanco wearing a traditional collar of arepas to celebrate his victory in the 2002 Vuelta a Colombia. 'Don Juan' went on winning in Colombia and Europe for an astonishing 20 years. His first Vuelta a Colombia was in 1991, when he was 21. He was a domestique, supporting Pablo Wilches in that race. Wilches won the race but was subsequently disqualified for doping! Don Juan was still going in 2009, coming up to his 40th birthday, still chasing that elusive 5th victory in the Vuelta a Colombia. *Photo Hernán Vanegas*

## 2003. Niño

In 2003, he abandoned the race after a fall and this time it was the turn of Libardo Niño, from Boyacá, who stormed up the Loma de Escobero on the 5th stage to take the leader's jersey, which he held all the way to the finish.

So the stage was set for the showdown between José Castelblanco and Libardo Niño in 2004.

12. Palacio was a plane spotter as a boy.
13. Just means Escobero Hill, a tough climb of 931metres vertical gain, ending with a fine view over Medellin.

Vuelta a Colombia 2003: Libardo Niño with guardian angels? At any rate, José Castelblanco crashed and Niño went on to win the race. *Photo Hernán Vanegas*

WHOSE TURN IS IT ANYWAY?

# 2004-2006 “It’s my turn! Whoops, no it’s not”

## 2004. ~~Castelblanco~~ Niño

And showdown there was. Libardo Niño won the opening, short time trial. José Castelblanco took the 5th stage and the jersey. During that stage, there was a tragic accident during a pile-up of the peleton, and a young rider called Juan Antonio Barrero was killed.

On the penultimate stage – a time trial round Bogota – Castelblanco and Niño were equal in time, just five seconds behind the leader.

Winning this race would put Castelblanco in the Vuelta Hall of Fame as a four times winner, alongside Cochise and Herrera.

Castelblanco did win the time trial, and went on the next day to win the Vuelta. But his joy was shortlived. A test taken after the race showed him to be positive for the banned hormone, testosterone. He was disqualified and handed a two year ban.Libardo Niño was declared the winner and the race records amended, deleting Castelblanco’s results. Castelblanco’s teammates came in second and third.

## 2005. Niño again!

A year later, Libardo Niño was back on the starting line for the 2005 Vuelta. Castelblanco was still on the bench (more precisely, in his farmhouse in Boyacá, surrounded by potatoes). The major threat to Niño was from Castelblanco’s old friend and team-mate, Buenahora, and his team. But four of Buenahora’s domestiques tested positive for illegal substances after the first stage and were disqualified!

At this point, Niño must have fancied his chances. But Buenahora showed extraordinary tenacity, riding solo for most of the race and taking the leader’s jersey with four stages to go. Exhausted but driven, Buenahora won the final time trial and had a slender lead of 3 seconds going into the final day.

Libardo Niño had déjà vu on the start line of the stage. It was just like the year before, when he and Castelblanco had started the last day neck and neck, 5 seconds behind the race leader. It was an unwelcome memory. Niño had lost that day and only Castelblanco’s subsequent disqualification for testosterone had brought him victory.

The final stage was normally a festival for the crowds in Bogota. A chance to cheer their man, wherever he had come in. The riders would ride 16 times round a 7 kilometre circuit, a ceremonial occasion modelled on the parade along the Champs Elysee in the Tour de France.

Not today. Anything could happen, and it did. With just 3 of the 16 laps to go, Buenahora had a puncture. With no team-mates to lend him a bike (because they had been disqualified, on Day One), he dropped out of the peleton. By the time he remounted, he was alone on the street. His rival Libardo Niño was 55 seconds ahead, sheltered behind his team-mates. It was an impossible gap. He abandoned and Niño won his third Vuelta.

After his disqualification for doping in 2004, Castelblanco had retired to his farm up in Umbita. But the itch would not leave him. Buenahora, his old Kelme and Selle Italia team-mate, persuaded him he could make a comeback.

So he got back into training, lost 10 kgs and lined up for the 2006 Vuelta, along with Buenahora. And his old rival, Libardo Niño.

## Farce in San Cristobal

The 2006 Vuelta started that year in San Cristobal, Venezuela. On the eve of the start, blood tests showed that over half of the contestants had red blood counts exceeding 50%. Normally an athlete with such a high count would be suspended, under suspicion of using EPO or some variant.

But 50%? You couldn’t disqualify half the race! It was a disaster that threatened the reputation of the Vuelta and Colombia cycling. After frantic discussion, the failure mark was moved to 60% and the samples were destroyed!

# Libardo Niño Corredor

## Born

26 September, 1968
Paipa, Boyacá
2,525 metres

## Early days

Libardo Niño was brought up on the altiplano of the Cordillera Oriental, with a sister and two brothers. His parents were farmers. When he was 18, he saw his uncle Israel race by in the 1987 Vuelta and decided to follow the peleton himself, all the way to Sogamoso. He arrived an hour after the finish and cycled home in the dark. But it was a start. With his uncle's support, he won several local races and then in 1992 he won the Novice award in the Vuelta a Colombia. He was briefly in the two Colombian teams Manzana Postobon and Café de Colombia and when they were dissolved he joined Kelme, the Spanish team.

## Career

He was a domestique in Europe without significant results, but when he came back to Colombia in the 2000s, he really started winning. He won the Vuelta a Colombia three years in succession: 2003, 2004 and 2005 (he finished second in 2004 but awarded the prize because his great rival José Castelblanco tested positive for testosterone on the penultimate stage). He himself tested positive for EPO during the time trial at the Pan American Games in July, 2007 and was later barred from competition for 2 years. He took part in the Vuelta a Colombia 2 weeks after the Pan American games and finished 5th.

## Vuelta a Colombia stages: 7

## Vuelta a Colombia podium: 3

He also competed in the RCN Clásico 12 times, victorious in 2005.

## Grand Tour & otherwins

None.

## Later days

In 2011 he was again sanctioned for a positive EPO result during the Vuelta a Colombia in 2010. This time the UCI banned him from racing for 8 years, and also annulled his results from 2010.

2006-2008

# They shall never die

## 2006. Buenahora Castelblanco

There was a retest the next day and six riders still failed but the remainder cycled on, including Niño, Buenahora and Castelblanco.

Niño started well. The first stage was a time trial which he won. But by stage 5, a new power had pushed his way to the front: the 20 year old Fabio Duarte who held the yellow jersey for 4 stages. But Buenahora and Castelblanco were still in there, fighting for every second.

Hernán Buenahora won the time trial up the Alto Escobero and put himself back in the jersey. But a blood sample taken that day showed excessive hematocrit, and he was not allowed to compete the next and final day.

Instead the overall winner was his team mate José Castelblanco, who had been disqualified for testosterone abuse 2 years earlier, letting their rival Libardo Niño in. So Castelblanco won his fourth Vuelta at the expense of his friend Buenahora, and joined the Vuelta Hall of fame. He was to spend the next five years looking in vain for a 5th win.

## 2007. Botero

Hernán Buenahora and José Castelblanco were back for the 2007 Vuelta, riding as usual for the Loteria de Boyacá. It was a senior team: Buenahora was now 40 years old, and Castelblanco, 37. Another Loteria rider was Israel Ochoa, who was 43. They were up against the comparatively youthful (34) Santiago Botero, recently returned from Europe.

Astonishingly, these four riders trounced the younger generation, taking the first four places. Right behind them was Libardo Niño Corredor. A few days later he tested positive for EPO at the 2007 Pan American games in Brazil and was banned for 2 years. You might wonder why he did not test positive in his home country during the Vuelta a few days before.

## 2008. Buenahora. Baez

Buenahora & Co were lined up against some heavy competition

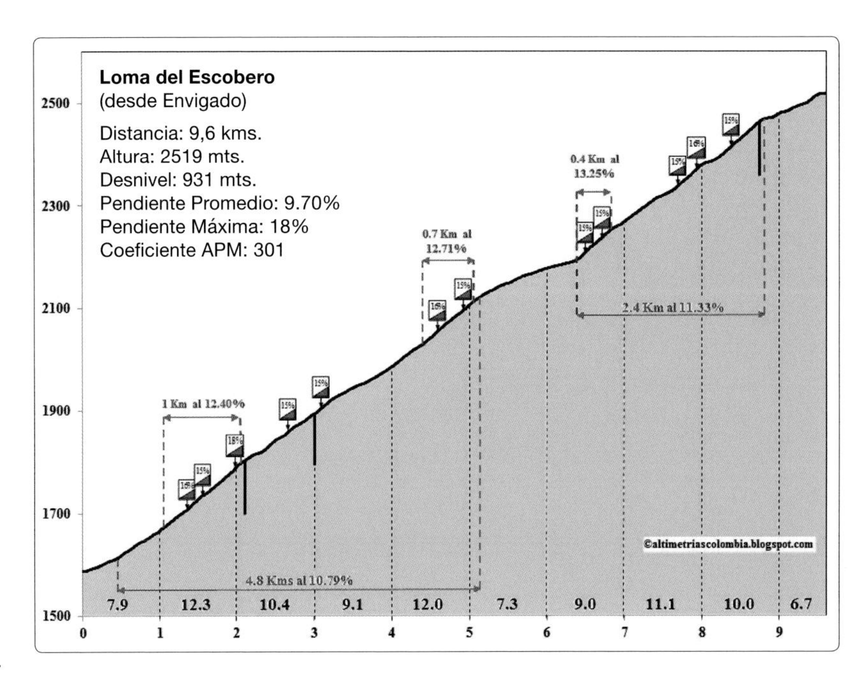


The Loma de Escobero makes the perfect hill climb for the Medellin spectators.
*Altimetria Alps&Andes.com*

at the start of the 2008 Vuelta, for the field now included three riders recently retired from Europe with serious Grand Tour credentials.

First, the Colombian Santiago Botero. Botero had been winning in Europe since 1996. He was King of the Mountains in the Tour de France of 2000, a first for any Colombian rider. Between 2000 and 2002, he had won 3 stages of the Tour and 3 stages of the Vuelta a España, and in 2002, he became World Champion in the Individual Time Trial.

Next was the talented Spanish rider Oscar Sevilla. Sevilla had also done well in Europe, having won the 2001 "Under 23" jersey in the Tour de France and come second in the Vuelta a España.

And third, Colombian Victor Hugo Peña, nicknamed "El Tiburon", the shark[14], because of his prowess as a swimmer (as a teenager, he was national champion in several water disciplines).

14. Victor Hugo Peña celebrated his swimming achievements with a shark tattoo on his left shoulder.

Long standing rivals Libardo Niño and Hernán Buenahora ascending the Alto de Letras.
*Photo Hernán Vanegas, El Colombiano*

2008-2009

# The Rock Racing trio

He had been the first Colombian to wear the yellow jersey in the Tour de France (2003), which he held for 3 days. And he had stage wins in the Vuelta a España and the Giro.

Victor Hugo Peña was the only one of the three[15] who had not been sanctioned or banned for misbehaviour in Europe. The other two had been implicated in Operacion Puerto, the investigation by the Spanish Police into the doping ring masterminded by Dr Eufemiano Fuentes. As a result, Botero had been dropped by his team T-Mobile, and banned from the 2006 Tour de France.

Tour de France 2003: Victor Hugo Peña became the first Colombian to wear the yellow jersey (here being interviewed by a smiling Hector Urrego).
*Photo Mundo Ciclistico*

But Buenahora was too good for them. He rode a superb race and came second. Unfortunately, he then tested positive for ephedrine, a decongestant which had the effect of expanding the veins and improving the flow of blood and hence oxygen to the muscles.

He was banned for two years. Another five cyclists (including two stage winners) also tested positive and were banned.

To general amazement, the 2008 Vuelta was won by an amateur, Giovanni Báez.

PS. Buenahora served his ban, and returned to the Vuelta in 2011, aged 44, and finished a creditable 16th.

## 2009. The foreigners are back!

The following year (2009) was a washout, as far as the Colombian public was concerned, literally and metaphorically. The ninth stage was controversially abandoned after a ferocious downpour led to landslides across the route. (See photo overleaf). The Venezuelan José Rujano was in the lead at that point, and he went on to win the GC. The sprints were won by another Venezuelan, and the "regularity"prize by a Spaniard – Oscar Sevilla!

It was the first time since the Spaniard José Gómez del Moral's victory in 1957 that the race had been won by a foreigner.

15. Perhaps it was mutual self-defence or just friendship, but shortly afterwards all three of them joined Tyler Hamilton in a new US team, Rock Racing.

Santiago Botero, Victor Hugo Peña and the Venezuelan José Rujano looking mightily upset during the 9th stage of the 2009 Vuelta. The torrential rain caused a landslide which delayed the start by 2 hours. When the organisers said "go" the peleton refused. There might be another landslide. The stage was abandoned. *Photo Juan Antonio Sánchez*

WHOSE TURN IS IT ANYWAY?

# 2010-2012 The UCI is not amused

## 2010. The Libardo, Sergio and Oscar show

In 2010, Libardo Niño was back, having served the 2 years ban imposed after testing positive at the Pan American Games in 2007.

Unfortunately, he tested positive for EPO during the Vuelta and this time was banned for 8 years!.

The main excitement of 2010 arrived after the finish. The race itself was a bit dull. Between them Sergio Henao (23) and his Spanish team-mate Oscar Sevilla (33) wore the tricolour jersey every single stage except for one. Sergio Henao won the GC and Oscar Sevilla came second.

But no! Shortly after the finish, Oscar Sevilla was disqualified. He tested positive for HES (hydroxyethyl starch), an anticoagulant substitute for blood plasma which can mask the taking of EPO by reducing haematocrit readings.

The legal battle over his disqualification and suspension went on for 18 months (Sevilla's defence was that the substance had entered his bloodstream as a result of emergency medical treatment after a fall), but the UCI eventually upheld the verdict (doping) and the sentence. Whether to show its displeasure or for some other reason, NO rider in the race was given UCI points that year, even though the race was officially part of the UCI Continental circuit.

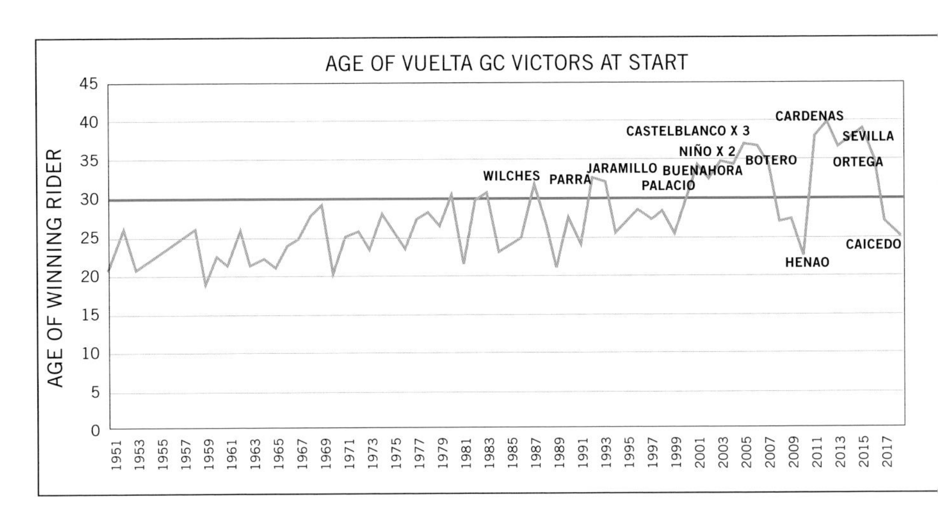


Before 2000, GC winners of the Vuelta a Colombia were almost all under 30. After 2000, they were almost all over 30.

## 2011-2012. If at first you don't succeed...

The 2011 and 2012 Vueltas were won by another senior rider returning from Europe, Felix Cardenas. Cardenas had ridden for Kelme – one of the teams implicated in Operacion Puerto – back in 2000 and 2001, and he had been riding in the Vuelta a Colombia for 15 years. Until 2011, his best years were in 1999 and 2003, when he made the podium and was King of the Mountains.

He was 37 when the 2011 Vuelta kicked off, and in remarkably good form. He was up against Oscar Sevilla and his young team-mate Sergio Henao (Sevilla was still riding, still fighting the disqualification and ban from the year before). Cardenas took the lead early but lost it to Sergio Henao. On the last day, a tough time trial which climbed from Medellin to Santa Elena, he was decisively quicker than Henao and took the overall victory.

Sevilla won two stages, and would have placed 5th, but these results were later annulled as part of the UCI sanctions from the previous year.

Sevilla was finally allowed back into road racing in 2012, and promptly set about showing what he could do. He won the Clásico RCN that year, for the second time.

14th August, 2014: Felix Cardenas celebrates as he wins the 8th stage of the Vuelta a Colombia, aged 41. It was his last professional win in long international career which included victory in the Vuelta a Colombia in 2011 and 2012.
*Photo Julio César Herrera*

In 2014, Oscar Sevilla powered up the Alto de las Palmas to win the 2014 Vuelta a Colombia by just 1 second. *Photo El Colombiano*

# 2013-2016 The Sevilla years

## 2013. Sevilla

The next year, 2013, Sevilla won the Vuelta a Colombia, in a strong field that included the victor of the previous two Vueltas, Felix Cardenas. Also in contention were Alex Cano, a young rider who had spent two years with Colombia es Pasión and his team-mate Mauricio Ortega. Sevilla took the leader's jersey with two stages to go and kept it to the finish. Alex Cano was second and Mauricio Ortega third. Felix Cardenas retired.

## 2014. Sevilla

In 2014, Oscar Sevilla repeated his strong late form. He started the final day just 2 seconds down on the leader, Fernando Camargo. But he won the time trial up the Alto de las Palmas, beating Fernando Camargo by 3 seconds and so won the Vuelta by just one second.

## 2015. Sevilla

The next year, he was again in second place on the last day, 28 seconds behind the leader and favourite, Mauricio Ortega. Ortega had been in the leader's jersey for six days and with just one day to go, seemed likely to finish wearing it. Again, the race finished with an individual time trial, from Medellin up to the Alto de las Palmas. And again, in a sensational finish, Sevilla simply blew away the competition, completed the 17.5 kilometres 1 minute and 29 seconds quicker than Ortega, and so won the Vuelta by 61 seconds.

## 2016. Ortega at last!

The following year, 2016, Sevilla won the Clásico RCN for a third time, and looked unbeatable in the Vuelta. As in past years, he came into the last day in second place, just 4 seconds behind Mauricio Ortega. The race finished in the big square in the Boyacán capital of Tunja. After four circuits of the town, Sevilla and Ortega raced uphill, neck and neck for the line. Sevilla won by 3 seconds. 4 – 3 = 1. After some intense deliberation, the judges did the maths and gave the overall victory to Ortega. Unbelievably, after many years of trying and at the age of 35, Mauricio Ortega had won the 2016 Vuelta a Colombia... by 1 second!

It seems clear that between 1998 and 2016, the Vuelta a Colombia – and domestic competition in Colombia in general – degenerated into the pantomime we have documented in this chapter. Old riders with long histories of doping have taken the prizes. Young riders are forced to dope to compete, or quit, or never stand on the podium. The authorities and most of the cycling press seem caught up in a frenzy of washing their hands while looking hard the other way.

In researching this book, we spoke to the manager of the anti-doping unit of Colombian cycling. He has been collecting samples for 20 years. Had he seen a lot of doping?

*No, not at all. It isn't common here. There have been some positive samples, but they've all been medically justified. I've never seen a positive sample where they've actually had to sanction the cyclist.*

It's difficult to find his words reassuring.

The doping control cabin at the 2018 Vuelta a Colombia. *Photo: Pamela Gowland*

Perhaps as the old guard finally retires, things will improve. The winners in 2017 and 2018 returned to the norm, at least in terms of age. Aristobulo Cala and Jonathan Caicedo are both in their twenties.

But the Vuelta is no longer the place where the best young cyclists in Colombia compete. In the new, international cycling world, the younger generation has (fortunately for us and them) found ways of being swept up directly onto the international stage, upon which they have achieved dramatic success. The roots of this transformation go back to 2006.

# The golden trophy of the Quimbaya

The Vuelta a Colombia trophy has been modelled on the ancient pre-Colombian Quimbaya poporo (one of the many gold artifacts stored in the Gold Museum in Bogota). Poporos were used to store lime powder, which was mixed with coca leaves and consumed during religious ceremonies.

The Quimbaya poporo *© Stephen Norman*

Michael Angel López celebrates victory in 2019 Tour of Colombia, holding the poporo trophy. *Photo Getty Images*

# 2006-2010 Colombia is Passion

In 2006, a new team was created in Colombia, with the public and specific objective of riding clean – and winning abroad. Sponsored by the Ministry of Trade, Industry and Tourism, and a major corporation, it was called *Colombia es Pasión*.

And in a rare fit of good judgement, the minister in charged picked an outsider called Ignacio Velez to run it. Velez was a modernist, a Stanford educated geek who loved data and who had experienced first-hand scientific American athletic coaching. Even better, Velez (shortly to be and still known as El Coach) passionately wanted his riders to ride clean. Velez hired Luis Fernando Saldarriaga as chief coach (shortly and still known as El Profesor) and Luisa Fernanda Rios as general manager.

Velez, Saldarriaga and Rios set about building a new, elite structure. One of the first challenges was to find a way to convince a sceptical world that the team WAS clean. They introduced their own version of UCI biological passport, and hired a private lab to implement it.

Velez, Rios and Saldarriaga went looking for new talent. Their objective was to build a team that could compete and win abroad. This was not just about prestige. It was a sensible strategy simply for winning races. Because to win clean, they needed a level playing field and Colombian domestic racing was about as level as the Loma del Escobero.

Fortunately for them, the uplands of Colombia had a new crop of prodigious talent, ready to be trained and set loose.

One of their first recruits was Fabio Duarte, a young Colombian rider who had come in 4$^{th}$ in the 2006 Vuelta a Colombia. He was riding against the Buenahora-Castelblanco partnership but still wore the leader's jersey for 5 stages.

In 2008 he joined *Colombia es Pasión* and won the Under-23 World Road Racing championship in Varese, Italy. The next breakthrough came in 2010.

## 2010. Back to the future

The Tour de l'Avenir (the tour of the future) is traditionally the race where the best young riders in the world announce their arrival. The Tour d l'Avenir in 2010 was stacked with names that would become famous. The American world pursuit champion Taylor Phinney, John Degenkolb from Germany, Tom Dumoulin, Mikel Landa and Michael Kwiatkowski, Romain Bardet and Michael Mathews, among others.

The Colombians included three *Colombia es Pasión* riders – Darwin Atapuma, Jarlinson Pantano and Nairo Quintana.

The penultimate stage was hilly, finishing with a climb to Risoul in the Alps. The three Colombians got into the breakaway, and with four kilometres to go, the 20 year old Nairo Quintana attacked and dropped the rest. He won the stage by 39 seconds, a big margin. The next and final day was a time trial and here Quintana triumphed again, winning by 47 seconds over the 13.5 kilometres course.

Quintana took the top spot, Jarlinson Pantano was third and Darwin Atapuma was ninth.

It was a huge result, the best that Colombian riders had achieved in the Tour de l'Avenir since the 1980s, when Alfonso Flórez had triumphed in 1980, and Martín Ramírez in 1985.

TV footage celebrating the international achievements of Colombian riders from 1960 to 2014.

If the prospects for the next generation are to be judged by the Tour de l'Avenir, then Colombia is in a good place. Esteban Chaves took first place in 2011. In 2012 Juan Chamorro came second, just 1 second behind the Frenchman Warren Bargueuil. In 2014, Miguel Angel López won, followed in 2018 by Egan Bernal. Add it up! In 9 years, young Colombians have won the Tour de L'Avenir four times!

# Doctor in the house

Dr Camilo Ernesto Pardo Poveda. *Photo Camilo Ernesto Pardo*

Dr Camilo Ernesto Pardo Poveda has been supporting and caring for Colombian cyclists since 1980. As the young medic of the Fusagasuga cycling club, he met the 17 year old Lucho Herrera. They are still friends. After that he was hired by the Colombian Cycling Federation and spent time in France during the '80s with the Café Colombia team. More recently he was team doctor to 4-72 Colombia, the team run by Ignacio Velez which was dedicated to clean cycling.

**Is it interesting, being a doctor to a cycling team?**

Yes. More than interesting! I have been fortunate to have looked after most of the great cyclists in this country at some time, since 1980. Lucho Herrera, Fabio Parra, Oliverio Rincon, Alberto Camargo. Oliverio Rincon in the '90s. And then the Colombia es Pasión guys...Nairo, Pantano, Sebastián Henao, Sergio Luis Henao, all were in my care. The only ones I've missed were Rigoberto Urán, who is great personal friend of mine. And Egan Bernal.

**How did you get started?**

I joined the Fusagasuga Club, as an aficionado. Lucho had just started. The club was riding in a competition the day I graduated. I just rushed out of the car, grabbed my diploma and went back to the race!

**Speaking in medical terms, why are there so many cycling champions from Colombia?**

There are many factors. Altitude is paramount. In Boyacá at 2600 metres we routinely see natural haematocrit (% by volume of red blood cells) levels between 50 and 55%. At 3000 metres, even more. This gives the athlete a natural advantage for the exchange of oxygen, both in the lungs, and cardio-circulatory. I mean delivering oxygen to the muscles. Essentially living at altitude has similar physical effects as doping by taking EPO. So altitude is one factor.

**Do you need to be raised at altitude to have these natural advantages? And do these elevated hematocrit levels persist when these athletes go to lower terrain?**

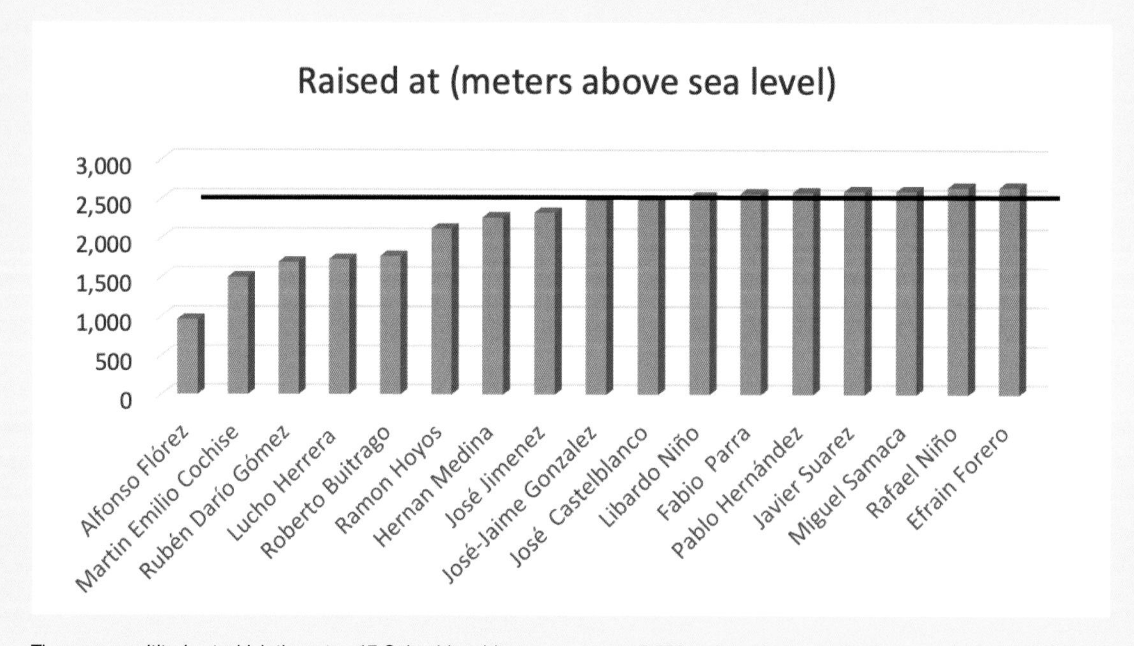


The average altitude at which these top 17 Colombian riders grew up was 2,206 metres above sea level.

next left page

2012-2015

TOMORROW BELONGS TO ME

# Colombia is Passion

So much potential, so much success. It seemed as though not only Colombian riders, but Colombian teams could succeed abroad, even with their limited budgets.

In 2012, buoyed up by the success of *Colombia es Pasión*, the minister of sport decided to put more money behind the project. Bizarrely, the minister decided to give the job of managing the expanded team to an Italian, Claudio Corti, rather than Velez, Rios and Saldarriaga. The new team was called simply Team Colombia.

The new venture was not a success, and folded in 2015. The tales surrounding this miserable episode reverberate around the cycling fraternity of Colombia today[16]. It is said that despite his multi-million dollar budget, Corti made his riders buy their own kit, even their bidons. That he put his son (an Italian) on the team, and took them training in Northern Italy in January, where they shivered with cold and missed their families. The team coaches were mostly Italian and the team luggage, while magnificent, sported the Italian flag!

Meanwhile, Vélez, Ríos and Saldarriaga pursued their dream with independent sponsorship, creating a team called 4-72 Colombia. In March 2014, in a defiant gesture to the rest of the Colombian sport, they and two other national teams, Orgullo Antioqueño and GW, published a manifesto entitled *Por un ciclismo ético* ('Towards as Ethical Cycling'). The manifesto proclaimed their determination to protect their riders' health and safeguard their right to compete in honest, legal and transparent sport. This included a Code of Commitment to which all three teams had subscribed, which made whistle-blowing obligatory and provided for education in anti-doping and sporting transparency.

But the collapse of Team Colombia meant there was no national team to compete overseas. The new and talented youngsters of Colombia voted with their feet.

16. Lots more detail about the Corti period and the story of the rebirth of Colombian cycling will be found in a forthcoming book by Matt Rendell, "Colombia es Pasión!: how Colombian young cyclists came of age".

12 **DEPORTES** — DOMINGO, 7 DE ABRIL DE 2013 — el**COLOMBIANO**

**CICLISMO** INFOGRÁFICO

# Quintana y el vuelo del cóndor

Pocos son los ciclistas que rompen el lote en la escalada. Con Nairo volvió la raza de los escarabajos.

Por **PABLO ARBELÁEZ RESTREPO**

Desde hace 20 años se dice que los escaladores dentro del ciclismo son una raza en extinción.

Los famosos dinamiteros del lote hicieron las delicias del público y siempre fueron tenidos en cuenta dentro de la categoría de héroes.

Con el accidente sufrido por *Mauricio Soler*, el 16 de junio de 2011, el lote mundial perdió a uno de sus últimos referentes en la escalada. Hoy quedan pocos, apenas unos cuantos que sean capaces de marcar diferencias, pero desde Colombia llegó la nueva sangre. *Rigoberto Urán, Sergio Luis Henao y Nairo Quintana*, tres de los más fuertes cuando se trata de las cuestas más escabrosas y empinadas.

Nairo, boyacense de 23 años, se cita en todos los ámbitos tras sus excelsas presentaciones en la París-Niza, la Vuelta a Cataluña y la Vuelta al País Vasco, competencias del World Tour de la Unión Ciclista Internacional.

Uno de los secretos para que a Quintana le vaya tan bien en la escalada de las altas cumbres, es que nació y se crió a más de 3 mil metros sobre el nivel del mar. Y que su capacidad de consumo de oxígeno es mayor que la del rutero promedio.

"La fortuna, es que Nairo se adapta tanto al frío como al calor. Lo veremos en el Tour de los 100 años al lado de *Alejandro Valverde*. Hoy es el número dos del equipo, pero en un futuro cercano, con mayor experiencia, de seguro será el uno, porque sus condiciones de escalador le darán ese puesto", analiza el técnico nacional de ruta *Jenaro Leguízamo*.

El mismo Valverde, hoy capo del Movistar Team, elenco en que está el colombiano, comentó en días pasados, que Nairo ganará algo grande en el ciclismo mundial. Porque está cercano al vuelo del cóndor ■

*"A Nairo le favorece su cuna. Desde pequeño se habituó a la labores rudas y esta es una garantía".*
**LUIS FERNANDO SALDARRIAGA**
Fue su técnico en Colombia es Pasión

*"Su capacidad es natural, pura, y adelanta un proceso de excelencia. Su relación peso-potencia es altísima".*
**IGNACIO VÉLEZ**
Creador del Colombia es Pasión

*"Tiene condiciones innatas. Proviene de los 3 mil metros de altura sobre el nivel del mar".*
**JENARO LEGUÍZAMO**
Seleccionador nacional de ruta

**FORTALEZAS**

- Trepador de los que cuando se va... se va
- Cuando la cuesta se empina cada vez más, es mejor para él.
- Maneja un buen sentido del ritmo en competencia.
- Tiene las piernas más largas que el tronco.
- Escalador inspirado, rompedor y consistente.
- En la alta montaña rompe, sostiene y cambia de ritmo.
- Corredor ganador y con notable mentalidad.
- De los ciclistas colombianos más técnicos sobre la bicicleta.
- Es de los pocos escaladores natos del lote World Tour.
- Posee un nivel de ventilación muy alto, por encima del promedio.

Nairo Alexánder
**Quintana Rojas**

Altura: 1.67 metros
Grasa 5.5 %

**Edad:** 23 años
**Peso forma:** 55 kg.
**Equipo:** Movistar Team de España
**Campeón:** Vuelta al País Vasco.
**Victorias de etapas:** 9 en Europa, entre ellas tres del World Tour (Dauphiné, Cataluña y País Vasco).
**Ranquin World Tour UCI:** puesto 4°, con 182 puntos

**DEBILIDADES**

- Le falta mejorar algo más la contrarreloj individual.
- Está en pleno período de maduración deportiva.
- Tiene una asignatura pendiente: cumplir el proceso como capitán de equipo en Europa.
- Le faltan competencias del World Tour que sólo el tiempo le dará.

**Lugar de nacimiento:** Cómbita
BOYACÁ

**LOS MEJORES ESCALADORES DE LA HISTORIA**

1. **FEDERICO M. Bahamontes** (España)
2. **CHARLY Gaul** (Luxemburgo)
3. **MARCO Pantani** (Italia)
4. **JULIO Jiménez** (España)
5. **LUCHO Herrera** (Colombia)
6. **EDDY Merck** (Bélgica)
7. **JOSÉ M.** Fuente (España)
8. **LANCE Armstrong** (E. U.)
9. **FAUSTO Coppi** (Italia)
10. **CLAUDIO Chiapucci** (Italia)
11. **LUIS Ocaña** (España)
12. **RICHARD Virenque** (Francia)

**Otros:** Alberto Contador (España), Bernard Hinault (Francia), José Rujano (Venezuela) y Joaquim Purito Rodríguez (España).

**MEJORES ESCALADORES DE COLOMBIA EN LA HISTORIA**

1. **Lucho Herrera** (Cundinamarca)
2. **Patrocinio Jiménez** (Boyacá)
3. **Mauricio Soler** (Boyacá)
4. **Rafael Niño** (Boyacá)
5. **Hernán Medina** (Antioquia)
6. **Javier Suárez** (Antioquia)
7. **Ramón Hoyos** (Antioquia)
8. **Norberto Cáceres** (Boyacá)

**Otros:** Chepe González y Oliverio Rincón (Boyacá), Martín Farfán (C/marca), Fabio Parra (Boyacá), R. Urán (Antioquia).

Foto: cortesía Movistar Team. Gráfico: Departamento de Infografía (N3)

Nairo Quintana: a legend in his own time and an inspiration to every young Colombian cyclist. *El Colombiano*

# Doctor in the house

from previous left page

Yes and yes. There are physiological changes to the body that come from being brought up at altitude. Nairo [Quintana] for example has exceptional lung capacity.

Another factor is that 80% or 90% of our cyclists are country folk. In the Colombian countryside, the bicycle is used a lot for transport. So from the time of Zipa Forero, and Ramón Hoyos and Cochise, lads in the countryside wanted to be like them. On their bikes. There were local competitions in small towns and from the early days the trainers and coaches went out talent spotting.

Our climbers are naturally trained and developed due to the mountainous terrain. For example, when Lucho [Herrera] started, he lived up halfway up a mountain road called San Miguel. No way to get anywhere except by going up or down! Nairo [Quintana] was brought up at the top of the pass near Combita, but he cycled to school every day. It was 16 kilometres but more importantly, the school was 700 metres lower. That's great training.

**Is it all about climbers then?**

No. From 2000 onwards, we started looking at the flat also. And at riders who could migrate from the flat to the velodrome. We've already found talent like Rigoberto Urán, and the sprinters, Fernando Gaviria, Nelson Soto, Sebastián Molano, Álvaro Hodeg. They have all passed through our hands. Now we diversify more. We are looking at all terrains, and also at time trials.

**Can we talk about doping? On Stage 19 of the 2018 Giro, Chris Froome cycled alone for 80 kilometres, and destroyed Tom Dumoulin's chances. What do you think?**

Look, probably the budget of the World Organization for doping control does not even match what a high-ranking cyclist earns. There are exclusive laboratories, not only for cyclists, for soccer, tennis, for all sports specialized in going forward of the controls. Now they are controlling EPO, but growth hormones, they can't detect those easily. And when they can, there will always be some new technique. The big teams, whether they are football, tennis or cycling, have the money to buy these drugs, so the difference between those big teams and the smaller teams is increasingly noticeable. It is a scandal. These are delicate subjects but we cannot cover the sun with a finger.

**Several Colombian cyclists have been caught doping recently. Why do they take the risk?**

For the results. To get a contract for next year.

Going back to Chris Froome. He claims he needed his bronchodilator because of his allergy. Well, I notice that at the Olympic Games in Athens, almost 80% of athletes suffered from asthma. So they all need bronchodilators! Clinical laboratories play an important role here because it is they who determine what test result implies an unacceptable level of medication. So a big team can get the laboratories to endorse their level of medication. But a small team can't, they can't afford it. So the big teams will go on, getting better than the rest.

Until someone dies.

**Dies? Have people died from their medication?**

Yes. Many have died. They tell you that they had a heart attack but they do not tell you the cause of the heart attack. Starting with the British cyclist Simpson who died of an overdose of amphetamine, there are many cases in which cyclists die of heart attacks. And there are athletes who had kidney problems and have required transplants, because of the medications.

**Are today's races more or less dangerous than before?**

You mean accidents? Speeds have greatly increased. Cochise's Hour record was 47 kph and now it's 60 kph! Similarly in the peleton. But safety factors have improved also. Helmets. When I started, you could race

Many Colombian riders pray for the protection of the Virgin before the race. *Photo Humberto Arango*

without a helmet! Bikes are more precise, more controllable now. The roads are better.

**What do you think of disc brakes?**

Very high risk. We have already several cyclists with sharp wounds caused by disc brakes. I think it will not progress.

**What other medical issues do you see?**

In the 1980s, the ratio between the front chain ring and the cassette were different. Say 53/42. That takes a lot of force to turn, so we had tendinitis, Achilles tendinitis, patellar tendonitis, quadriceps. Now we have say 36 or 38 on the front and large cogs on the back, 28/30/32. Less load and easy to change gear so the incidence of tendonitis has decreased.

With increased speeds, what we see are fractures, abrasions, everything that is trauma. And respiratory infections have always been frequent due to changes in temperature. For example today we left San Gil which is 600 metres above sea level and we went to almost 3000 metres. From hot to cold.

We also have gastro-intestinal problems. If you are from Boyacá, you eat certain types of food. When you go to the coast, the food is completely different.

The regime of our cyclists is super strict. We manage 5 menus. I design them. When we are in one region, we ask for this, in another one we ask for that. We try to change the recipes to keep it interesting. Our biggest problem is fish. We have had a lot of trouble with the fish because the fish from Vietnam, the pangasius, comes loaded with mercury and they pass it off as robalo or snook. We stick to trout!

**What are the most difficult moments of your career?**

I have seen the death of several cyclists in accidents. I have seen two accidents that left the cyclist there, stone dead. One, a cyclist arriving on the road from Pereira to Manizales. He crashed before Chinchina, against the rockface. Another coming down from Bogotá to Girardot by Alto de Rosas. That was into a car – a Land Rover – which had a hard steel mesh in the front. There the head was embedded. Those were the most dramatic, the rest are fractures.

There are accidents in all races, but the riders are religious. Paisas [Antioquians] are devoted to the Virgin of Carmen. Those from Boyacá and Sogamoso pray to the virgin of Morca. They say she appeared in Morca, which is a village near Sogamoso and the cyclists are devoted to her. Even the young ones. There are others who pray directly to God. Every morning before the race begins, before the technical talk, we pray an 'Our Father', and an Ave Maria ... always.

# The courage of Juan Pablo Villegas

Juan Pablo Villegas. *Photo Klaus Bellon, Alps & Andes*

Juan Pablo Villegas was born on 15$^{th}$ October, 1987, in the little town of Pacora, high in the mountains of the Central cordillera. It is coffee growing country, and Juan Pablo came from a long line of coffee workers.
As a child, he hauled coffee and plantains in the fields. When he was 11, he started working full time, getting up at 4.30am to walk to work, often carrying loads of 70 kgs uphill. Somehow he managed to study as well and graduated from high school.

His father would recount stories of the great Colombian cyclists of the past, and then in 2001, he saw the Tour de France on TV. As he rode his old mountain bike around Pacora, he dreamed of cycling glory.

He was lucky. He rode in some local competitions, and someone saw his strength and helped him. In 2011, he joined **Colombia es Pasión**. It was an amazing team, with a line up of stars destined for international success: Nairo Quintana, Esteban Chaves and Jarlinson Pantano, among others. **Colombia es Pasión** was committed to riding clean, and very public about it. Villegas did well, and in 2014, he won the Tour of Mexico. But in 2015, the team lost its sponsor, and had to disband.

Juan Pablo Villegas did not have a foreign team waiting to sign him up. His choice, as he saw it, was between joining a Colombian team and doping, or going back to the coffee plantations.

In a brave and outspoken interview with Klaus Bellon on the AlpsAndes blog, he explained his decision, starting with a dramatic claim:

*...when I first joined [**Colombia es Pasión**]. Nairo was there, Esteban Chaves, Pantano, it was just an amazing amount of talent, all with internal testing, with a huge focus on clean sport, and strong ethical component to the team. A team of guys who, we can see now, are capable of winning big races among the best in the world. And yet, that year in the Vuelta a Colombia the best guy in the team was maybe 18$^{th}$ in the GC. So that data point should serve as your answer. We won nothing, not even top ten.*

*In races in Colombia our best rider could sometimes lose 20 minutes in a stage. In the GC, our best rider would be 30$^{th}$.*

next left page

# 2016-2017 Colombia is Passion

They fled into the arms of the big Grand Tour teams. Nairo Quintana went to Movistar, Fernando Gaviria to Etixx – Quick-step, Pantano to IAM, Darwin Atapuma to BMC, Esteban Chaves to Orica Greenedge and Miguel Angel López to Astana.

And they were welcomed, because the foreign teams had also figured out that Colombia was full of young talent which – with the benefit of professional coaching – could rapidly become world class.

In the course of 24 months, a whole generation left the domestic scene and became cyclists on the world stage. They earned a lot more money, more prestige and just as important, they earned real UCI points.

They did not – at first – come back and race in Colombia. Their new teams had no interest and professionally there was little to be gained.

Why? Because of the dominance of the UCI, the Union Cycliste Internationale. This organisation, which was founded in 1910, has become de facto the governing body of cycling worldwide, partly through the UCI points system.

The points system categorises both races and riders, and the classification of one affects the others.

Riders are given points based on their performance. 500 points for winning a Grand Tour outright, points for each stage win, points for the King of the Mountains and the intermediate sprints. And so on. But not all races are equal, naturally. It is presumably a lot harder to win a Grand Tour than a regional road race, and the UCI system reflects that.

The points awarded to the winners of a given race determine its status in the professional world and its attractiveness to the competitors, and their sponsors. Likewise, the number of points a rider makes in a year determine his or her international ranking, and are a significant indicator of their status and value.

But although the UCI claims a worldwide mandate, it favours European races, partly because there were and always has been, genuinely more of them. The total points on offer from races in Europe in the year 2000 was 34,000. The total points on offer from races in the Americas (including the USA) was 4,000. There were similar disparities with Asia and Africa.

Dramatic revival of Colombian road cyclists since 2010. *Data from ProCycling.com*

There is some logic to the UCI's position: they will upgrade the points awarded to a race, depending on the calibre of the riders who ride in it. Which of course is measured in UCI points! So race organisers face a chicken and egg problem: to attract great riders, they need their race to be worth more points. But to make it worth more points, they need to attract great riders.

So ambitious young Colombian riders are desperate to ride in Europe. In Spain, for example, there are no less than 53 UCI events with points. In the Americas, just 3. And this after strenuous lobbying in recent years.

# The courage of Juan Pablo Villegas

Vuelta a Colombia 2018. Random testing has not lifted the curse of illegal drug use from the domestic peleton.
*Photo Stephen Norman*

from previous left page

Juan Pablo did not go back to coffee farming, or at least not yet. He had an offer from an American team, Smartstop, which was dissolved after a year, and then he was back in Colombia with Manzana Postobon, the reformed successor to **Colombia es Pasión**. And things must have improved, because in 2017 he won two podium places in the 2017 Vuelta a Colombia.
But it was not a happy experience.
There were those in the peleton and the media who resented his whistleblowing. He was threatened on and off the track, and the next year he decided to hang up his shoes for ever.

You could say that Colombian cycling has suffered twice from the curse that is doping.

The first time was in the 1990s, when Colombian riders in Europe found themselves suddenly unable to win races against a new breed of European supermen. Especially supermen who could climb mountains. Riding clean, the Colombians could not compete. The result was disappointment back home. The press and the public needed new heroes after Parra and Herrera, and they weren't getting them.

**"If you can't beat them, join them."**
Colombian cyclists in the foreign teams learned about EPO, blood transfusions and so on. When they returned to Colombia, they brought these bad habits with them, and so in a different way, the domestic sport suffered. Where the UCI was finally driven to get a grip on professional doping, at least on World Tour teams after the Lance Armstrong revelations, the Colombian Cycling Federation, the Colombian press, the domestic teams and their riders remained stuck. They learned bad habits late, but kept them later.

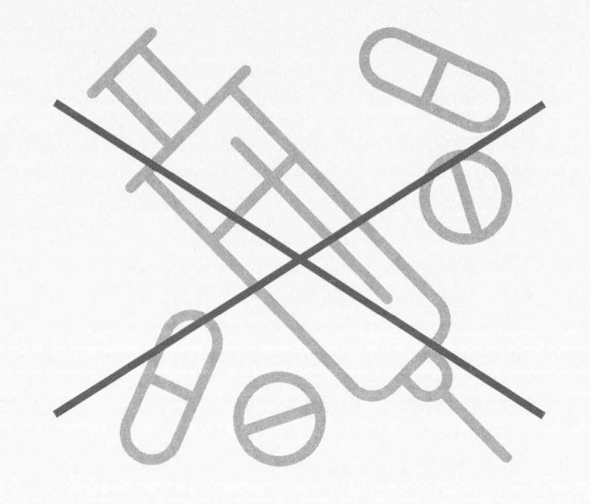

2018

# Meanwhile, back at home...

Particularly galling – and damaging – for the organisers and sponsors of Colombian races like the Vuelta, was that for a time, the Vuelta and the RCN got NO UCI points at all.

Lacking a national team, without any influence over the big international teams, it was impossible for the Colombian Cycling Federation to put the Vuelta back on the international map. But they had another idea[17].

17. According to some sources, it was not their idea. A Colombian cyclist had the idea and found the money. He approached the Federation to bless it with the UCI. Instead, they adopted it.

3rd stage, Tour of Colombia 2019: Excited spectators leap to catch a pink bidon thrown by a rider. *Photo: El Colombiano*

## 2018. The Vuelta Oro y Paz

In 2018, the Colombian Cycling Federation and the UCI approved a new race, the Vuelta Oro y Paz (the Tour of Gold and Peace), then renamed the Vuelta a Colombia 2.1 and now simply the Tour of Colombia 2.1.

This race has a number of interesting features. In the first place, it is a UCI Continental event, with a rating of 2.1. This means points. For example the GC winner receives 125 UCI points (there is still room for debate: the winner of the Vuelta a España receives 850 points and of the Tour of California 399!). Second, the race takes place early in the year, in late January. Third, it is shorter than the Vuelta, with six stages. And finally it is run in Colombia at altitude. Good for the hematocrit levels!

The combination of these four factors made the new race highly attractive to international teams looking for early season altitude training.

The Colombians on the Sky (now Ineos) team persuaded their management to enter the inaugural event, held in early February 2018, and so did Nairo Quintana and the Movistar team. Two other WorldTeams competed: EF – Education First and Quick-Step Floors, as well as three national teams and a dozen continental teams.

The inaugural Vuelta Oro y Paz created an excitement in Colombia that had been missing for a generation. The crowds at each finish were simply ridiculous.

The race was a six day parade of Colombian talent. The power of Fernando Gaviria – perhaps the Cochise of his day – took the leader's jersey for the first 3 days, before handing it over to his team mate, the Frenchman Julian Alaphilippe, just for one day. Then Rigoberto Urán won the 5th stage but Nairo Quintana took the pink jersey.

On the final day, Egan Bernal started just 10 seconds behind Quintana. The Sky team put Tao Geohegan Hart and Sebastián Henao into the breakaway. With 3 uphill kilometres to go to the mountain finish at Manizales (2,160 metres), the youthful Bernal launched an attack and the others supported him all the way to the line. He won the GC by 8 seconds. Consolation for Nairo was that his brother Dayer won the stage.

There was general celebration and generosity of spirit reminiscent of the early days of the Vuelta a Colombia. As Cycling News put it:

# Cycling for all

Women's racing in Colombia predates Lycra and helmets: (see next page).
But today, there are more women cycling in Colombia than ever before, partly as a result of social change and progressive moves like the Bogota and Medellin ciclovias.
For many years, the authorities have closed major roads in the city to traffic on Sundays. In Bogota, some 1.7 million people, (about a quarter of the city's population), head out on their bikes every weekend.

There are more sportives and cycling competitions for women, as well. In 2006, the Cycling Federation introduced "The Tour Femenino" which runs along the same course as the road race for young men, the Vuelta del Porvenir. It is a race open to all comers and is not UCI recognised.

The Colombian star, Carlos Vives, sings of his love affair with his country – and his bike.

"When we grow up, we're going to beat them…"
*Biblioteca Publica Piloto, Medellin*

A decade later, the Federation created a new race, confusingly called the Vuelta a Colombia Femenina. This is a 5 day race which follows the same routes as the Vuelta, but shorter. The new race was a great success and in 2017, the Federation announced that it would in future be recognised as a UCI 2.2.3 event.

Both races have been dominated in recent years by one outstanding woman, Ana Cristina Sanabria, who won the Tour for four years in succession (2014 – 2017) and the Vuelta Femenina for all 3 years of its existence to date (2016 – 2018).

After winning the Vuelta Femenina for the third time, Ms. Sanabria followed in the footsteps of her male colleagues and joined a foreign team, in this case Swapit Agolico, the only Grand Tour team from Latin America. More recently, Paula Patiño, a rising star who finished 6th overall in the 2018 Vuelta Femenina, joins the eminent list of Colombians who have signed up with Movistar.

It is too early to say whether female cyclists will achieve the same eminence in competitive cycling as their male colleagues, but the omens are good.

Lima, Peru. 9th Aug, 2019. Mariana Pajon wins the BMX gold medal in the Pan American Games.
*Photo Martin Alipaz/EFE/Alamy Live News*

María Luisa Calle is a professional cyclist with a long and successful career in on the road and the track. She won a bronze medal in the 2004 Summer Olympics, and in 2011 she won a gold medal in the individual time trial at the 2011 Pan American games, at the age of 43. (Sadly, at the 2015 Pan American games she tested positive for the growth hormone GHRP2 and was banned for 4 years.)

In addition to a strong field in road cycling, there are great Colombian female riders in other events.

On the track, Juliana Gaviria (sister to Movistar star Fernando Gaviria), Diana Maria Garcia and Martha Bayona Pineda have won numerous international medals in the team sprint and the keirin.

Mariana Pajon is the reigning Olympic BMX champion, winning gold in the women's BMX event in the 2012 London Olympic and then again in Rio in 2016.

# 2019 Meanwhile, back at home...

*Even if it was impossible to move – Nairo Quintana needed 20 police and security officials to get him from the podium to his bus – it was impossible not to be infected by the sheer joy of it all.*

*There was a visceral wave of noise when Bernal, Quintana, Urán, and points jersey winner Fernando Gaviria were called out onto the podium, followed by hearty chants of their names. As Urán said, even the foreigners from the smaller teams had been roared over the line, most of them unable to stifle their smiles.*

For 2019, the race was re-branded the Tour of Colombia 2.1. Quintana, Bernal, Gaviria, Atapuma and Chris Froome all took part.

And what of the Vuelta a Colombia? It will still happen every year. Jorge Ovidio Gonzales, President of the Colombian Cycling Federation, told us this:

*La Vuelta a Colombia is the traditional event of Colombian cycling, this event is 68 years old and is for cyclists living in Colombia, for those who are not in Europe and for those who want to finish their sporting career in our country; the Tour Colombia 2.1 is a completely international event, only for UCI teams and national teams, it is the real Colombian cycling event..*

We would prefer to say that the Vuelta has had a daughter who will perhaps surpass her mother. But while the Tour of Colombia is welcome, it does not fix the domestic issues, and especially the 20 years old culture of doping and the old boy network that has so resolutely refused to tackle it.

However, in 2018, the government appointed a new Director of Coldeportes. An elite squash player himself, Ernesto Lucena exudes youthful energy. Armed with his charm and his budget (which funds the Cycling Federation, and through it the Vuelta and the Tour), he is attempting a series of reforms to energise and clean up the domestic scene. On the doping side, Article 380 of the criminal code will be revamped to criminalise the supply of non-addictive drugs like EPO and its derivatives. The drug testing lab in Bogota will be recertified by the UCI and will be widely used, starting with amateur races. The Federation will be encouraged to reform itself, to become financially transparent and to provide better support to the cycling clubs. The Tour of Colombia will be extended in length and scale. And beyond that, who knows?

Lucena dreams of the Vuelta rejuvenated and a national pro-cycling team riding again up the Alpe d'Huez. In Colombia, as they say, cyclists spring from under every rock in the mountains. 1,600 teenagers aspire to ride in the Vuelta del Porvenir de Colombia each year. So the raw materials to make Lucena's dreams come true are even more abundant now than they were in November 1950, when Efraín Forero pursued his dream across the Alto de Letras and descended, triumphant, down to the astonished citizens of Manizales.

This one minute clip provides poignant images of 22 year old Egan Bernal with his teammates riding into Paris to win the 2019 Tour de France. © ASO

Ladies at the start (date unknown). *Biblioteca Publica Piloto, Medellin*

Pintuco
SUPERIOR A LO MEJOR

Horacio Gil Ochoa rejoiced in timing and co-incidence.
Here, the photographer's art has captured the statue,
the girl, the ox, all perfectly in line, all looking at the cyclist.
*Biblioteca Publica Piloto, Medellin*

*May the road rise up to meet you,*
*May the wind be always at your back.*

*May the sun shine warm upon your face,*
*And the rains fall soft upon your fields.*

*And until we meet again,*
*May God hold you in the palm of His hand.*

Irish Blessing Prayer

*For Gui*